What They Saved

What They Saved

Pieces of a Jewish Past

Nancy K. Miller

University of Nebraska Press | Lincoln and London

Library of Congress
Cataloging-in-Publication Data

Miller, Nancy K., 1941–
What they saved: pieces of a
Jewish past / Nancy K. Miller.
p.   cm.
Includes bibliographical
references.
ISBN 978-0-8032-3001-9
(cloth: alk. paper)
1. Miller, Nancy K., 1941- —
Family. 2. Jews—United
States—Biography.
3. Kipnis family. 4. Jews,
Moldovan—United States—
Biography. 5. Jews—Mol-
dova—Chisinau—Biography.
I. Title.
E184.37.M56A3 2011
929'.209476—dc22
2011007977

Set in Scala & Scala Sans
by Bob Reitz.
Designed by R. W. Boeche.

For Vivian Liska

Contents

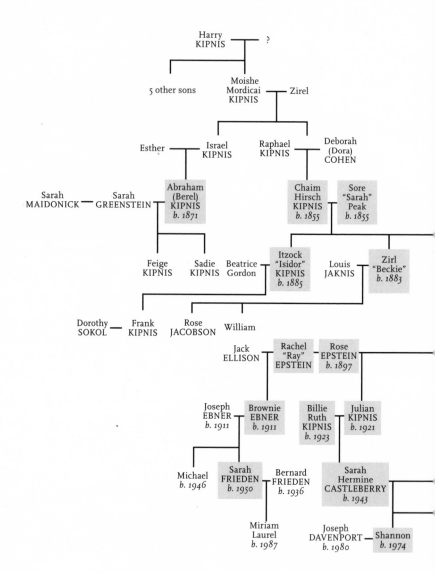

The Kipnis Family

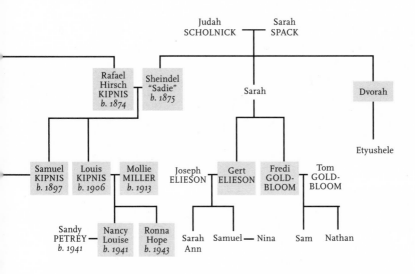

Judah SCHOLNICK — Sarah SPACK

Rafael Hirsch KIPNIS *b. 1874* — Sheindel "Sadie" *b. 1875*

Sarah

Dvorah

Etyushele

Samuel KIPNIS *b. 1897*

Louis KIPNIS *b. 1906* — Mollie MILLER *b. 1913*

Joseph ELIESON — Gert ELIESON

Fredi GOLD-BLOOM — Tom GOLD-BLOOM

Sandy PETREY *b. 1941* — Nancy Louise *b. 1941*

Ronna Hope *b. 1943*

Sarah Ann

Samuel — Nina

Sam   Nathan

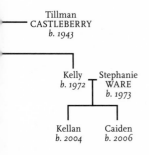

Tillman CASTLEBERRY *b. 1943*

Kelly *b. 1972* — Stephanie WARE *b. 1973*

Kellan *b. 2004*   Caiden *b. 2006*

part 1

How I Found My Family in a Drawer

1. The Heiress

When my father died, I became a middle-aged Jewish orphan. It's not that I wasn't already Jewish, of course, or that I set out to say Kaddish for him—I had no idea how to do that, even if it had been a daughter's place. But now that the last keeper of my Jewish past was dead and I was free to put it behind me, I started worrying about the future of my Jewish self.

As I began to take stock of my father's affairs, I found, tucked away in his bureau drawers and in the many compartments of the Danish modern credenza in the dining room that had become his home office after illness forced him to retire, the unsorted memorabilia of our family. Slotted into the red wells, the rust-colored file folders that for years had traveled with him on the long subway ride between our apartment on the Upper West Side and his office on Wall Street, I found (as I expected) a cluster of pale manila folders, containing the dated remains of cases from his practice as a lawyer in Manhattan. But I also found baffling items from a Jewish legacy I knew almost nothing about: a formal family portrait glued to crumbling brown cardboard, with a fully bearded, fedora-topped patriarch seated in the front row next to my grandfather; a receipt for the upkeep of a cemetery grave in Queens; directions to an unveiling; copies of handwritten letters that appeared to be in Hebrew; an embroidered blue-velvet tallis bag (complete with tefillin); a folder mysteriously labeled "property in Israel" (including a map); and tightly curled locks of dark-blonde hair packed into a cardboard box that once held fancy French soap.

My sister readily relinquished her claim to this puzzling cache of random Judaica that had accumulated untouched for decades in the cluttered rooms of the rent-controlled apartment where my father had spent the last seven years of his life, mourning my mother as he vanished into the debilitations of Parkinson's disease and finally the fog of dementia. My sister, who was passionate about jazz, instead took home the contents of the Louis Armstrong file, one of my father's two claims to minor celebrity. In the 1940s he had been Lucille Armstrong's adviser and confidant when she was looking for a divorce from her famously wandering husband.

Without knowing why, I saved it all.

After the death of my parents—and as I thought, inevitably, about my own death—I became possessed by a drive as strong as the one that had led me to hold on to what had already been saved, a drive to figure out what had happened before me. The collection, however eclectic, pointed to a specific enough elsewhere, a map of meaning and relations that nonetheless eluded me. These strange things provided clues, almost an invitation, to follow where they led. Their original owner was gone, true, but I now had in my possession objects that offered hints about the missing narrative, a story about an immigrant family of pogrom orphans (that much I knew—they had come because of the pogroms, a refrain remembered from childhood). But what had happened to this family that had come to America from Russia and then vanished without a trace? Or maybe that was exactly wrong. This family, over generations, had no doubt left discernible traces—in objects, and documents, and finally in me. I could feel that mute history like a deposit in my body, without being able to say how, a feeling made more intense, paradoxically perhaps, by the fact that I had no child who would in turn inherit the objects from me.

A few years later, when I moved to a larger apartment, I took the boxes out of storage. I had become the custodian of this repository, but was it worth the sacrifice of an entire closet? Not that I thought making room for what I privately called my archive was, on the face of it, extravagant. I had already filled one closet with my graduate-school notebooks, term papers, and drafts of old love letters I could not bring myself to jettison. What was I keeping all that for?

Missing—entirely, it seemed at first—was a way to reach into the silence that surrounded these memory remnants. Early on, my husband's son, a scientist, asked me what my book was about. I told him that the things I have inherited are like signposts to a journey I cannot completely describe; I don't know enough to connect the dots between them. He offered a word he thought might help me, "spline." Splines fill in the blanks between isolated points, construct a complete object from limited information.

I was already captivated by the word when it cropped up again, a few days later, in a framer's shop. The shopkeeper showed me a narrow ridge of wood at the edges of the handmade frame I'd selected; it's a spline, he said. That's what holds the corners together. I'm a sucker for metaphors, and this one has my name on it, especially because it works in two directions: as a way to navigate unknown spaces and as a way to frame the fragmentary map of my discoveries.

Since then, I've conjured stories from my objects about the people to whom they once belonged. They've become evidence, telling details from a family history that was until now lost to me.

I say family history, but what I mean is my father's side, the Kipnis side.

There are always at least two sides to a family, and we grow up believing the mythologies that attach to each. We learn that we are like—take after—one side or the other. And each side tends to bear a label that explains or seems to explain who you are like, or which ancestor you favor, as the phrase goes: the nose, eyes, or hair of either parent or their parents. Especially when the inherited trait is unappealing, we derive a certain comfort in knowing where it comes from, the solace of resemblance. Others managed to make it through life with that hair—mine, my father's—the tribal topiary.

From the beginning, the deck was stacked in favor of my mother's side of the family, the Millers. For one thing, there were a lot of them—two living grandparents, my mother's three siblings and their children, my cousins. The brothers and sisters maintained family ties as long as their parents were alive to care for. But the Millers were all about success, which also meant that the siblings competed with each other, noting which of their families was turning out to be the richest (we were always the poorest). Their children—the six cousins—were pitted against each other, everyone looking to see which kids performed the best in school. Still, even when the original siblings succumbed to bitter resentments and mean feuds, they continued to pass on the cherished stories of their childhood. The time Uncle Al lost his leg hitching a ride on the Amsterdam Avenue bus, how Uncle Dave, the bachelor doctor and eldest child, supported himself in medical school by playing poker, how the girls—my mother, Mollie (the baby of the family), and her older sister, Fay—addressed envelopes to earn money that would help pay for Dave's tuition. The time my mother kept a sardine in her jacket pocket until it rotted and the smell ruined all the clothing in the hall closet. Embellished at every retelling, the stories had, as it were, a life of their own, eclipsing the dramas of our tiny household, which never reached the status of lore.

Family stories aglow with the aura of myth.

The Miller grandparents were immigrants from Eastern Europe, from Russia, as were the Kipnis grandparents. From where exactly, or even what their name had originally been, was never mentioned. In summer, when the siblings gathered to share an old Victorian house in Deal, New Jersey, Grandpa Miller, who was a master storyteller, would take the six grandchildren for a drive in his boxy, gray Packard and mesmerize us with tales of wolves howling in the forest, from which children like us—three boys, three girls—made a brave escape, laughing all the way home. Our mothers would complain to Pop that he was scaring us. It occurs to me now that we were getting the "Peter and the Wolf" version of tales of pogroms suffered by Jews who, like him, in their own youth had escaped into the surrounding forests, running from the Cossacks and fearing for their lives. But that history was never mentioned—if, indeed, remembered. At the time, being scared was the price we kids willingly paid for the thrill of sitting piled up together away from the parents, while our grandfather deftly manipulated the wooden knob at the top of the silvery stick shift.

My grandfather Willie basked in what Grace Paley called "the summer sunlight of upward mobility." The only reminder of his Eastern European biography lurked in the occasional slippage between "w" and "v"; his night-school English had banished the past into linguistic accident. When he presided over the Miller family seders, it seemed normal for him to be seated, propped up with pillows, in a large armchair, like the patriarch he was, ensconced in his role as storyteller and head of the clan. Smiling. He was always smiling. As far as he was concerned, his own story had turned out well. He was American; he even voted Republican.

My father's side, the Kipnises, first lost by numbers; there were so few of them. Two years before I was born, my grandfather died at age fifty-nine, "of disappointment," my mother said; he couldn't adjust to life in America. We never met my father's brother Sam, who had moved to Arizona because his son Julian suffered from asthma. I don't think I even saw pictures of them. Arizona seemed farther away than Russia.

The second reason for the shadowy status of the scrawny Kipnis branch (compared to the leafy Millers) was a vague sense of gloom attached to their lives. Grandma Kipnis, as we called her, lived in a small, dark apartment in the Bronx, and when my father brought my sister and me to visit her on a Saturday morning, it seemed to me that we had traveled to a foreign country by subway.

"You're so cold and selfish," my mother would say bitterly, exasperated by the stony silences I had perfected as a child. "You'll die like Grandma Kipnis, alone and friendless." I shrugged. I didn't even look like her. If my father had a rosier alternative to my mother's grim prediction, he did not offer it.

My mother waited for her mother-in-law to die before launching into her full repertoire of righteous indignation, tales of how she had suffered at the hands of a woman who could never be satisfied and made you know it. What could you expect from such a woman who in Russia, she said, rejected a suitor because of the cut of his boots? Somehow I always suspected, without understanding until much later, that my mother resented my grandmother's very being—and by extension, in posing our likeness, my own. I did not wonder then why she, and not my father, was the Kipnis native informant.

My grandmother's death, when it came, twenty years into my parents' marriage, changed the course of our family history, but it's only now, more than fifty years later, that I'm starting to guess how deeply. In almost every way, that death marks the crucial turning point in this story, a story about the extinction of my father's side of the family, that began with my grandfather's early death, my uncle's departure from New York, and the earlier disappearance (a banishment? a removal?) of my grandfather's siblings and cousins. With my grandmother gone, our family was liberated from the dissonant, foreign, unassimilated element she represented. Although my mother's own mother, Grandma Miller, was equally unable to speak English correctly and understand the world she lived in, my mother did not feel threatened by the immigrant past she embodied in the very fullness of her figure. My mother seemed to tolerate her existence because of her abiding love for my grandfather. He was the person and parent whom she wanted to please and whom she loved unreservedly.

My grandmother's death in 1954 coincided almost exactly with my father's one serious, newsworthy triumph as a lawyer. It was also the beginning of my parents' luxury-liner travels to Europe and of the acquisition of the trappings of upward mobility my mother had longed for. They were fully assimilated now. They could be tourists in the Europe their parents had fled and abhorred. Glamour and money had laundered the pogroms.

When his mother died, my father became an orphan at exactly the age I was when I later lost him. Not young at forty-eight, but not old either. At the time, of course, I did not think of him as an orphan, the way people were orphans in the Dickens novels he loved; but in his own way, I think he was. Except for the anecdotes my mother liked to tell whenever she was irritated with my father or me, the Miller waters closed around our little family when Grandma Kipnis faded completely from view.

In my thirties, buoyed by seventies feminism with its expansive dreams of self-reinvention, I swapped the family names and became a Miller. It wasn't exactly swapping. I eliminated the name of my ex-husband, which I had so eagerly added to my father's when we married (I was fashionably, if clumsily, hyphenated). I chose what looked like the clarity of the future. Miller. A name you'd never have to explain. I reveled in my new anonymity.

I didn't expect my father to die when he did. He had just recovered from a bout of septicemia contracted in the hospital and seemed to be regaining strength. I was scheduled to leave for a year's sabbatical in Paris when he died at home—on Father's Day weekend in June 1989. After the funeral I had ten days to take a last look at what remained of my parents' things, leaving the final sorting to my sister. How could I stay? It was my first sabbatical. My husband and I had sublet our apartment, rented one in Paris, and an entire chain of plans was already in motion. But not staying also meant that I lost the chance to know really, in detail, what I was leaving behind.

There was almost no one on my father's side with whom to share the news. I first called my father's cousin in Canada, who had visited him during his illness and whose kindness I had admired. Their mothers were sisters, and the cousins seemed genuinely fond of each other. I knew that Gert would be sad but that she would want to know. I assumed that my father's brother, Sam, being nine years older than my father, was probably dead; maybe somehow I knew that he was. I wondered about his son, Julian. I found an old résumé for Julian in the top drawer of the credenza, with a phone number in Tennessee. I reached his wife, Ruth, who surprised me by knowing who I was. "Oh, Lou's daughter," she said warmly. She regretted my father's death, though she had never met him, and she gave me a P.O. Box address in Magnolia, Texas, for Julian, who was now her ex-husband. I wrote to tell him about his uncle's death, but I never heard back. I filed the résumé though, for future reference, just as my father had.

As my sister and I sifted through the unidentified photographs (who was the formally dressed man on horseback?), we realized how little my father had ever said about his brother, his father, or even his mother, whom we had known, if our ceremonial visits could be considered to have bestowed a form of knowledge. We stared at the portrait taken in a Lower East Side studio where what appeared to be a large family, including our grandparents and a nine-year-old Sam, had come to pose together. But who were those other people?

When I returned to New York after my sabbatical, my husband drove my sister and me to the cemetery in Flushing to see my father's headstone. Instead of feeling finished with the family mystery, as we wandered through the maze of graves, I felt pulled to figure it out. I copied the mystery photograph and sent it to my father's cousin in Canada to see whether she recognized the people in the portrait. They were members of my grandfather Raphael's family, she supposed, but she knew nothing about them. In her letter, Gert volunteered some information about my grandmother's family—about a sister who had emigrated to Argentina—but fixated as I was on my grandfather's line, I was not yet interested in *that* other side. Still, I kept the letter, since that is what savers do.

In the first year of the new millennium, a decade after my father's death, a real estate agent from California contacted me about a parcel of land in Palestine that my father's mother, he said, had bought in the 1920s during the British Mandate. I was convinced that this was a clever Jewish con game. My grandparents lived on the Lower East Side when they came to New York, that much had registered. How could they have had money to invest in land? But as the man continued his pitch, I distinctly remembered a folder in my father's files labeled "Israel property & Sheindel Kipnis" in bold capital letters; "and Sadie Kip" was lightly penciled in at a later date.

The folder contained three cancelled checks from 1926 signed by my grandfather Raphael Kipnis; an inky blue surveyor's map with tiny numbered plots laid out like rows of tombstones; and an elaborate certificate of ownership for two dunams of land in the village of Souba, issued in my grandmother's name by the Palestinian government. There were also copies of an exchange from 1949 between my father and a family friend visiting Israel. The friend, a real estate lawyer, had looked into the matter for him: "The land is constantly increasing in value," he wrote to my father, "and your land is directly in the middle of the new plan for Jerusalem. If you don't need the money, my advice is to hold on to it for some time." The paper trail confirmed the evidence on the map but ended there. Had my father, who certainly needed the money in those years, sold the dunams, those two plots that each represented one-fourth of an acre? I had no idea, but I held on to the folder, just as my father had held on to the property, or so it seemed.

The realtor, a man in his late sixties, insisted that the dunams existed and that he could sell them for me. Collaborating with a colleague in Israel who specialized in identifying property belonging to absentee foreign owners, the agent guaranteed that cooperating with him would pay off handsomely. He didn't bother with estates that were worth less than $200,000, he said. The prospect of an inheritance was tantalizing. Still, I resisted. How could this be true? But the man's persistence wore me down. What did I have to lose, he asked, since I didn't have to write any checks? I began to assemble the documentation he needed to navigate the Israeli bureaucracy on behalf of the heirs.

It was too late to ask my father why his parents had bought the miniature parcel of land (did this mean they had been Zionists, something he always denied?), just as it was too late to ask him to identify the people in the family portrait, those ancestors whose name I had so lightly shed. So many troubling questions set in motion by the purchase of the dunams, questions that I had never found the time to ask.

But even if nothing came of it, no money from the dunams, that is, I would gain a story. After all, wasn't it a story about the Kipnises that I had been missing for so long?

2. Kipnis in Memphis

Ten years after vanishing deep into Texas, my cousin Julian had returned to Memphis with a new wife. I found him by dialing the number on the résumé, again reaching his ex-wife, Ruth. Once my cousin had been located and had authorized the real estate agent to represent the Kipnis heirs, there was, strictly speaking, no obligation for further contact between us, no requirement for us to meet. No requirement, but on my part an absolute compulsion. How could I not want to meet my father's closest living relative, his brother's son—his nephew and my first cousin, the only cousin from the Kipnis side? I wanted to know what he knew and what he remembered about what I didn't know. I wanted, above all, to know what had happened between the two brothers.

If Julian was surprised to hear from me, he didn't say so. He knew me nominally as my father's older daughter, of course—"you're the one who went to Paris." That remained my calling card, it seemed, where the clock had stopped on me some forty years earlier. When I described the situation about the property and the terms of the legal agreement, Julian joked that they should hurry up and finish the paperwork since he was almost seventy-nine, had already had two strokes, and was suffering from double vision. Preoccupied with his failing health, Julian was not especially eager to revisit the past beyond the business that had prompted the phone call.

Julian's daughter, Sarah, on the other hand, had just begun exploring the Kipnis side of the family on the Internet and, though a "novice on the computer," as she put it in her first e-mail, was ready to trade stories. She began with the only one I had grown up with, beyond those of the generic pogroms. It was about the Russian basso, Alexander Kipnis: "I do know that the family is supposed to be related to Alexander Kipnis, who was a great opera star. It was stated that the family disowned him because he sang for Hitler." I had not heard the Hitler part (which isn't true, though the singer had been under contract to the Berlin Opera until 1935), but like Sarah, my sister and I had also grown up with the belief that we were related to Alexander Kipnis. My father had a large collection of his recordings. Years later, when I met Alexander's son, Igor—a distinguished harpsichordist—I learned that all Kipnises claimed to be related to Alexander. It wasn't hard to see why the claim was appealing and suggestive: Alexander was famous, and he was born in Bessarabia, as were our relatives. He was only slightly younger than my grandfather. Yes, we *could* have been distant cousins, but we probably weren't. On the other hand, Sarah and I were related—first cousins once removed—and she was only a few months older than my sister.

We started exchanging photographs by mail—neither of us knew how to scan or send images yet—and comparing notes: the scraps of information, some erroneous, we had gleaned casually and separately over the years. "Let's see," Sarah began one morning in September via e-mail, "I think I have found something else." She had found Chaim, my great-grandfather and her great great-grandfather, the date of his arrival in the United States—July 25, 1899—and the address of his destination, 96 Allen Street on the Lower East Side. A great-grandfather! That's all it took, the baited hook of what Sarah called "the genealogical thing," to convert me from spectator to participant. I had to know more. I cashed in my Delta frequent-flyer miles and flew to Memphis.

As I prepared for my encounter with Julian, I studied the résumé for clues about his life. Under education Julian had listed a BS degree from the University of Arizona (no date but with the odd precision, "Instructed Mammalian Anatomy"); he had then studied engineering and law in the South, without getting a degree in either. After four years of military service, he subsequently spent four years as a CID agent (whatever that was). At forty-two, Julian described himself as being 71 and ¾ inches tall (way taller than my father, or his), with a ruddy complexion. He listed membership in both the Memphis Pistol Club and the National Rifle Association. For "Location Preference" he had written: "Will relocate and/or travel as the situation requires," and under "Reason for Change," a pithy summary: "No sufficient challenge remaining." Julian appeared to have had a career of sorts in business management, changing jobs almost every three years. He had also designed and flown a plane.

My cousin, the marksman.

Unlike my father and most of the people I knew in New York, whose careers had moved forward in straight lines, Julian's trajectory was plotted on an unfamiliar map that included Texas and Arizona in addition to Tennessee. But why was I so surprised? Why expect him to be "like us"? That was yet another proof of what my Alabama-born husband called "Manhattan provincial." After all, despite an abbreviated Bronx childhood, Julian had grown up in Tucson. Planes went with guns, and military service had capped Julian's coming of age in the Southwest, with its wide-open skies.

Julian was too ill to make the drive to the airport. Sarah, Ruth, and Sarah's twenty-six-year-old daughter, Shannon, were waiting for me at the gate. How would we recognize each other? I would be wearing black and looked like a professor. Sarah had told me that she was large—and that was true. Ruth was tiny and slender and resembled my Alabama mother-in-law; Shannon was buxom and bouncy, her dark straight hair pulled back in a ponytail. Sarah was wearing a large Jewish star around her neck; Shannon and Ruth, a gold cross. Despite these signs of difference, the generations of adult women seemed bonded in a palpable form of connection that I envied. I could not have replaced the trio with, say, my mother, my grandmother, and me in a comparable show of affection, except perhaps in the bright flash of home movies from childhood summers at the Jersey shore. I took a snapshot of the three women on the porch of Julian's ranch house in the suburbs of Memphis, where they deposited me for our meeting.

It was early October, but summer was hanging on. Ceiling fans were circulating warm, humid air. Julian's second wife, Jerry, a small, bustling figure in a powder-blue tracksuit, served us sweetened iced tea from a huge plastic container. Except for the iced tea, we might have been in Long Island, or any suburb where the furniture reflects an upholstered formality at odds with the casual dress of its inhabitants. Denim meets damask. Julian was wearing a guayabera over loose-fitting jeans.

We sat at a table in the living room, I with my notebook, Julian with a scrapbook of photographs and clippings. I had debated bringing a tape recorder but feared that might have seemed pretentious, or at least off-putting. That turned out to have been a wrong guess; Julian was more than happy to narrate his life story for posterity. Did we suspect that our interview was both the first and last conversation we would have? Neither of us acknowledged it.

"Bronx, asthma, nine years old." That was the only piece of information that squared with the rudimentary biography I already possessed. I was hoping to hear about the old days on the Lower

East Side, my uncle, our grandparents, whatever Julian might have retained of these people, whom he had known when they were relatively young and still close to the memory of their immigrant experience. As their first grandchild he might have heard stories from them—or from his father, stories about them that his father might have passed on. But all he said was that our grandfather Raphael had been a bookkeeper, that he was sweet (confirming what I already had heard from my mother), and that his father had talked about the Cossacks. No matter how persistently I tried to bring the man back to his New York childhood, what I thought of as the location of a shared, inherited history between us, and between his father and mine, he spiraled away from it to what interested him: the saga of his postwar life as a pilot and inventor.

But that's not exactly what happened. The next entry in my notes refers to his father, Sam, my uncle: "Dad: keeps books for Cotton Club"; I had drawn an arrow pointing from "Cotton Club" to "godfather": Dutch Schultz—"Beer Baron of the Bronx," a Jewish gangster nicknamed "The Dutchman." I could tell that Julian expected me to know all about him.

My uncle worked for a gangster! I kept scribbling, trying not to show the thrill that raced through my body. Sam had often taken the boy with him on his weekly visits to neighborhood stores. In the 1920s he had transported bootlegged beer in a horse-drawn cart, and then delivered the money he had collected to the Cotton Club. Yes, the gangster was his godfather, Julian continued, picking up his little white pug dog, whose square face, I had decided, also bore the traces of the Kipnis family line. Could the story be true? Lots of question marks on this page of my notebook. Julian's description of my uncle transporting beer during Prohibition in a horse-drawn cart strained credibility. But maybe that was precisely why I had never heard this piece of family history.

My cousin wanted to tell me his own life story, a great adventure he had already recounted in an unpublished autobiographical novel inspired by the Aldrich Ames spy case that had broken in the late 1990s. Only his wife had ever read the book. I asked if I could see it. Julian had sent it to a friend in another state for safekeeping—in case anything happened to him, he said in a lowered voice. But he divulged the novel's title, *Is Your Daddy Home?*

Julian nimbly skipped over the war years to get to the subject of the novel: spying, dealing with traitors. After the war he joined the oss, the precursor to the cia. He also (or was that the same thing?) belonged to a "unit of thirteen men not known to each other, a kind of hit squad," I find in my notes. "Killed seven people?"—a question mark in my handwriting, not even an exclamation point, and in brackets "finished one off with his hands." I took it all down, in a state of bewilderment.

The remainder of my notes summarize Julian's relatively ordinary career in business ventures in the South, except for one item: "shot in throat." Julian was shot in the throat? Later, Sarah filled me in on the backstory: a worker shot her father in the throat when he was the manager of a minority business making Levi's somewhere in Tennessee. The doctors could not remove the bullet. On the same page in my notebook is Julian's self-description: an "expert shooter in target and competition" and a "gunsmith." It was in the course of giving shooting lessons at a local pistol club that he met his second wife. At this point in the story, his wife nodded in vigorous agreement: "Kip," she interjected with admiration, "was a great teacher."

I kept trying to move Julian back into his childhood past.

Studying a photograph of him as a small child dressed up in a middy blouse and belted tweed coat as he stood on a city street with my father and grandfather holding a New York pretzel bigger than his hand, I said, "You were very cute." Not missing a beat, and not smiling, my cousin replied, "I still am." His wife refilled our glasses with the cold tea, nodded, and beamed. In the notebook I drew an arrow after that comment, pointing to my father's initials—my father, who at the end of his life flirted with his various caregivers and doctors; if nothing else, in old age the two men shared a survival strategy.

Reviewing his career, Julian seemed proudest of the plane he had designed, and he gave me a photograph of it, with him perched on the wing. In this picture of Julian as a slender young man, with cropped dark hair and sculpted cheekbones, I can easily see his resemblance to my father when he was young. The engineering skills that went into the design of his fighter plane were recycled in late life to enable the execution of more domestic feats. Julian had assembled an antique walnut grandfather clock, not from a kit, he specified, but from blueprints and flat lumber, and he had made a dollhouse with doll furniture for his new wife's great-granddaughter. Before we parted, my cousin additionally presented me with magic-marker drawings he had made of Don Quixote—black ink sketches on stiff white stock. I mailed them back to Sarah when I returned to New York, thinking that she might want them for her scrapbook. Perhaps "quixotic" was the adjective he would have chosen for himself, reflecting his quest for something that seemed to have eluded him all his life.

His wife pressed me to stay longer, but Julian was clearly tired, and we had run out of things to say. I was relieved when Shannon's car pulled into the driveway.

That night, I went to dinner in town at the Texas Roadhouse with my new relatives Sarah, Ruth, and Shannon. Clinking cold mugs of beer, we toasted our ancestors and our future inheritance. We marveled at the strangeness of our encounter; we were so different, and yet connected. The floor of the steakhouse was littered with shells from the bucketfuls of peanuts set out on every table. I resisted for a while and then, pressed by Sarah, gave in to custom, boldly brushing the shells from the edge of the table with the side of my hand. The food was good, and I was happy that we had not gone to the Roadkill Café, a restaurant Sarah had mentioned in an e-mail, praising its cuisine.

Was what Julian told me about being a spy true? I asked, sipping my second beer. Oh, Ruth said, with a slight smile, Julian always exaggerated. But Sam worked for the gangster Dutch Schultz? Oh yes, that was how he got his start in the restaurant business in Tucson. You know, liquor, food. I tossed more peanut shells on the floor. Maybe that was why Sam and my father had parted ways, a lawyer in the 1930s couldn't afford a gangster brother. After dinner we caught the timed spectacle of ducks parading across the red-carpeted lobby of the world-famous Peabody Hotel. As we strolled along the banks of the Mississippi in the early evening, I never felt more a New Yorker. The Hudson was my river of choice.

I spent the night at Sarah's, in Shannon's old room. Here in the suburbs of Memphis, as Sarah sifted through her box of pictures with me, I discovered that we had the very same family portrait that I had stared at and puzzled over so many times. The man with the black suit, sullen gaze, and untrimmed grizzled beard was our common ancestor: my great-grandfather, her great-great-grandfather, Chaim Kipnis. She showed me how to navigate "www.kipnis.org," a Web site that posted ship's manifests for all immigrants to America with our family name. So, it was true. They had come from there, and we had descended from that journey. I found myself wondering again—anxiously—as I had when I looked at the photograph after my father's death: who *were* these people I was related to, and what had happened to them?

I had traveled to Memphis to hear about Uncle Sam, about my immigrant grandparents, and about my father when they all lived in New York. I ended up instead with the family connection to a gangster, an installment of the missing story I could never have imagined.

That was my first lesson. *The hardest thing to find is what you think you are looking for.*

Because then there was Sarah, my newly found native informant. She wasn't much of a writer, she said apologetically when we met online, but she almost immediately proved to be a fluent e-mail correspondent. From the Kipnis Web site, Sarah had already retrieved the dates of my grandparents' and her grandfather's (my uncle Sam's) immigration to America. Not long after, she asked me the one thing I knew a little about: "Have you ever heard of a town called Kieshiniev in Russia?" Yes, I had, Kishinev was a city famous for a pogrom that shocked the world in 1903, but that was all my knowledge of it.

In the beginning I was simply following the impulse that had seized me when the phone call from the broker in Los Angeles jarred me into action. In the beginning what drove me was the longing for information about the Kipnis side of the family; I wanted to know whatever there was to know. By the end of my weekend in Memphis, I had already learned the second lesson of the quest. *You don't necessarily know what it is you'll want to know.*

3. The Report Card

The more I thought about Julian, the more confused I felt about his relationship with my father. Why had my father saved the résumé? Had the two men ever seen each other as adults in my lifetime? I returned to the drawer, to the handful of letters from his nephew that my father had saved, and started reading.

I say "the drawer," but of course, it has never been a single drawer. In the chaotic aftermath of my father's death, my sister and I walked through the rooms of the apartment to see what there was that we might want to hold on to, opening closets, emptying drawers. The credenza was of primary interest, but there were also my parents' dressers. We boxed, labeled, and set aside for storage whatever looked important, personal, or simply had handwriting on it, and marked the rest for sale or other disposal. But once I opened the boxes and transferred the contents for safekeeping into my own apartment, I lost track of where they had been in our parents' apartment. Now these intimate remains are stored in three drawers of an old-fashioned, glass-fronted secretary in my study, in no particular order.

I was startled to learn that Julian had visited my parents in the fall of 1961, when I was first living in Paris. "I can't help but repeat myself," Julian writes. "The trip to New York and the visit to you was the best tonic I've had in years. I wish we could have been closer in the past, that is close enough to help me break loose much sooner than I did—However, that's all in the past and will remain so." Nothing further in the letter illuminates the nature of their bond or fleshes out my cousin's cryptic references to a period of emotional turmoil. From the date, I guess that Julian means moving to Tennessee from Arizona, away from his own parents in Tucson. "Ruth would like very much to meet you," Julian adds, "now that I've explained to her that I really have a segment of the family that is truly civilized." My cousin proposes a guided tour of Paris, presumably conducted by my parents: "Would France tolerate four Kipnises at once?"

That fall, as I settled into my new life as a graduate student in Paris, I was desperately trying to get away from my parents. I was Jean Seberg fooling around with Jean-Paul Belmondo. When I wasn't Jean Seberg in *Breathless*, I was Jeanne Moreau playing the Marquise de Merteuil in *Les Liaisons dangereuses* (I was studying the novel at the Sorbonne). The last thing I would have wanted then was to meet a relative from Tennessee. I suspect that the speculative trip to Paris was no more than an exercise in *politesse* on both sides—a belated game of imaginary Kipnis family ties. Still, I'm struck by Julian's obvious fondness for my parents, and his gestures of self-revelation: "As I told you, I'm having trouble sitting still." This restlessness is probably the truest thing about the person in the résumé, the self-portrait of a man unable to square reality with his desires. At age forty, Julian is taking up a new "hobby": enrolling for a three-year extension-school course that will result in an LLB degree. "I do not intend to practice," he adds. The law school project gets added to the string of undated degrees. Perhaps it is also Julian's way of reconnecting with his uncle the lawyer, whom he hadn't seen since he was a boy in New York.

Looking for Julian I find my father in a trove of items from the 1920s: his high school report card, two copies of a playbill from a school play performed on "Class Day," a graduation program, a torn newspaper clipping about the performance, a cluster of family snapshots, and a school autograph book.

For a long time I viewed the contents of the drawer as belonging uniquely to my father, as traces of his early life that he wished to preserve. When I encountered objects that baffled me—unidentified locks of hair or photographs of strangers—I first looked upon them as markers of my father's efforts to memorialize his past. But little by little I started to have another idea. My widowed grandmother lived alone for twenty years in an apartment in the Bronx, where my father visited her regularly. I've come to think that when she died my father did what my sister and I did upon his death: gathered up whatever looked worth saving, without paying too much attention. In fact, what this probably meant was that my father often just *resaved* what his mother had saved, deliberately or not. Some of what I have assumed to be *his* might originally have been hers.

What I take to be my father's souvenirs may well be his mother's memory of her second son. This entire archive, this virtual scrapbook that I believed to be his, might well never have been his at all but rather a palimpsest of joint ownership, a chain of remembrance no one was willing to break: she saved, he saved, I saved. The doubt about provenance came to me forcefully whenever I tried to fathom the relation between Julian and my father. Midway through my reconstruction of their story, I realized that I was probably looking at the two of them through my grandmother's eyes. I can't know whether my father edited his mother's collection; I can't know if her ephemera is now promiscuously mixed in with his by his carelessness or mine.

Despite my intense desire to know the truth, however partial or incomplete, I am forced to recognize that the process of finding the story continues to change the story. As I advance into the territory of recovery, I can't trust even myself. That may be the hardest lesson of all.

At the top of the card from De Witt Clinton High School, June 1924, six months before his January graduation, my father

has added "M." and on the back of the card has doodled with signatures: "Louis M. Kipnis, Sec" and, more strangely, *"Julian Kipnis, LLB."* Why sign the name of his three-year-old nephew? Does he think that "Julian Kipnis" has a more glamorous ring than "Louis"? Does he fantasize that under his guidance Julian will also become a lawyer, and does he here show him how he would sign his name?

I study a snapshot of my father, smartly dressed in a suit and tie, holding Julian, who looks to be age three, in his arms.

My father seems pensive; Julian, with his Buster Brown haircut, happy and relaxed against his young uncle's body. I wonder how Julian, as a little boy growing up in New York, saw the two brothers—the one, his father, always at loose ends, picking up jobs here and there, including one for a well-known gangster; and the other, his uncle, setting out for law school.

There are at least half a dozen snapshots all taken against the background of the same chain-link fence, probably on the same June day. Ten years later the city would create Sara Delano Roosevelt Park at this very location. My father, in these snapshots, stands with his head tilted, practicing a look of elegant indifference. When the three Kipnis men pose together outdoors, they are all three in hats. Sam and Raphael sport straw bowlers, banded with a wide gros-grain ribbon. I note my father's crisply folded pocket-handkerchief, the bowler, and the lighted cigarette between his slender fingertips; the handkerchief continued, the cigarette did not. My grandmother, in a flapper dress adjusted to her fireplug shape, sausage curls piled atop her head, smiles, one arm jauntily akimbo. Two years later, Sheyndel (sometimes Sheindel), as she is still called on official documents, buys the two dunams of property in Palestine.

The story of the inheritance, we might say, starts here, next to the chain-link fence.

In addition to the high school report card and the group of images taken before the chain-link fence, I find an earlier artifact from my father's Lower East Side education: a bound, black-leather autograph book, with "Autographs" printed in gold script across the cover, from January 1921, the date of my father's graduation from PS 160 at age fourteen. Slipped between the book's multi-colored pages are the graduation program and an official black-and-white photograph of the school, Manhattan neo-gothic, with a pushcart on the corner. When my father graduates, his brother Sam, who has by now abandoned schooling for himself, trots out the fifth commandment (not that any of the other messages ring with originality) above his signature: "To Louis—Gain by my experience. Obey your father and mother. Your brother, Sam." Rose Epstein, who will marry Sam later that year, before Julian is born in December, weighs in just as formally on the following page: "To Louis, Think *right* and you will be *right*." A cluster of classmates sign off in a preview of today's texting style: "From a fellow grad-jew-8"; same pun minus the ethnic label: "grad-u-8." Of the list of 115 students in the all-boys graduating class, only 2 have non-Jewish names.

One day, scanning the page of the autograph book on which Sam has wished his brother well, I recognize for the first time the error I made when I was trying to decipher the scribbles on the back of my father's report card. The hand that signed "Julian Kipnis, LLB" was not my father's but his brother's. Sam, looking at his younger brother's report card from a fancy high school, imagines a future for his little son that will not resemble his own. Not only does this make more—much more—sense than my previous interpretation, but it also adds a poignant edge to all I will subsequently learn about Julian's life and sketchy career, and about the intense ties of identification between father and son, Julian and Sam, two men who, as Sarah would say, could never stick to one thing. This will not be the first time I will retrace my steps to confront the paradox of hiding in plain sight; it is yet another note from the field, moving back in order to move forward.

How many times have I missed what was right before my eyes?

Along with the report card and the program from the high school's graduation ceremony is an undated newspaper clipping that features a scene from the performance of *A Girl to Order*. My father appears under the stage name "Monroe Kipnis." Monroe, front stage, in a dark suit with a neatly folded white pocket-handkerchief, is playing Harold "Puck" Evans. The entire student cast has Jewish names and plays characters with WASP names and nicknames.

The poor quality of the newsprint makes it hard to read expressions clearly, but the tilt of my father's head in the class play resembles the pose in the snapshots. Louis M. seems to be distancing himself from the scene—the limited stage of his life. It's as though he is already elsewhere and someone else. Maybe this dreamy reserve translated in adulthood into a certain untouchability, an unavailability that prevented us as children from ever knowing for sure what went on behind the smiling mask.

I'm in love with this urban archaeology, enamored of my artifacts: the report card, the school play, the snapshots, and the luck, in this case, that my father's high school was considered newsworthy at the time. I'm able to place the report card and clipping, literally fragmentary evidence, frayed around the edges, into the broader cultural archive in which they fit. A scholarly article, for instance, describes the population of De Witt Clinton High School as a melting pot: "An extremely diverse yet selective student population epitomized both the potential for immigrants to overwhelm American civilization and the hope that meritocratic education offered the smoothest path to assimilation." I slot my slender, adolescent father into this narrative, an ethnographic surround for Louis M. Kipnis on the "smoothest path" to success.

Twenty-five 4½ x 2½ inch photos, almost half a deck of cards, which they resemble, of my father engaged in a variety of outdoor activities with other men in uniform; and two even smaller ones, 2 x 2½ inches, of my father boxing with a sparring partner. What to make of this clutch of loose images, without date or identification? I often stared at these snapshots with a kind of bewildered amusement. In these tiny, now pale beige snapshots, my father has never been more handsome, an almost adolescent beauty that was gone by the time I knew him. I have trouble connecting my earliest memories of my domestic, domesticated father with this young man—in uniform—an incarnation of masculinity. But there he is, smiling, clowning, posing; he is definitely posing, suavely at ease with guns and cannons and pitched tents. I had never heard of my father doing any kind of military service, and yet what was this, if not military? I thought the images might be from the New Deal ccc (Civilian Conservation Corps) camps, but my father's youthfulness didn't fit their dates. Nothing turned up under his name when I searched the available government records of military personnel.

I would look at the snapshots, marvel at them, and replace them in the drawer. One day I made a date at the Graduate Center, where I work, with a colleague and biographer, David Nasaw, an expert on twentieth-century American history and culture; surely he would know, or at least point me in the right direction. He recommended a senior researcher at the New York Public Library, a few blocks from our building on Fifth Avenue, a man profiled in a *New York Times* article as "The Library's Helpful Sage of the Stacks." The "sage" referred me to a specialist in genealogy, Warren Platt, who solved the problem almost instantly by searching the *New York Times* archives for my father's name. (Lesson: *Never skip the first step.*)

The headline from the *New York Times*, July 19, 1927, announced, "2,000 Youths of Three States Ordered to Report at Citizen Training Camps." Now that I knew what I was looking for, it was not difficult to find more background from the period. A call for applicants, published in the newspaper several months earlier that year, described the ideal candidate's qualifications for the program: "Young men between 17 and 24 years, who are physically fit and of good moral character, are eligible for enrollment." The camps had as their mission not so much to form soldiers as to provide lessons in citizenship and duty to country. The inventors of the Citizen Training Camps designed the summer event as "all expenses paid" and offered instruction in athletics, including "baseball, swimming, handball and other games." But the finale, at Fort Hancock, New Jersey, where my father was sent, included "working with the big guns that constitute part of the defenses of New York City." So, in August 1927, at age twenty, my father, still using his invented middle initial (M.), headed out to Fort Hancock for his thirty days of training.

Of course, it was not all baseball and swimming: there were military activities, camping in tents, sleeping on folding cots, learning to use weapons. Oddly, the one image that my father enclosed in a cardboard frame (pre-stamped "Souvenir from") is not a snapshot but a tintype, and it pictures my father rinsing underwear—an undershirt, as near as I can make out—in a basin near a pump, next to a fellow citizen in training. Maybe he wanted to show his parents that he was a good son and could take care of himself away from home. Why had my father answered the call? Perhaps he was attracted by the all-expenses-paid month in the country. Or perhaps he had a childhood memory of his big brother's uniform from his service in World War I.

I don't know what my father did between graduating from De

Witt Clinton High School in 1925 and completing Brooklyn Law School in 1929. I remember his explaining that "in those days," you could go to law school without first going to college, which is what I assumed he had done. He graduated from City College after World War II, with the flourish of Phi Beta Kappa. But what my father was up to in the interim was a question mark—until a discovery I would make when I had almost finished this book solved the puzzle.

I return to the chain-link photos and consider my cousin Julian, the old, ill man I met in Memphis, looking at him in this extended family that surrounded him as a child—doting grandparents, loving parents, handsome young uncle—trying to connect the dots, to fill in the blank spaces of the great unknown canvas of my lost family, the spline.

On November 16, 1930, Julian writes to his grandparents from his new address at 1571 Macombs Road. "Dear grandpa and grandma," the boy's clear, round script, in pencil, on lined notebook paper, proudly announces his accomplishments as a nine-year-old: "I am feeling well and hope to hear the same from you. I am going to school every day. I know my work pretty well. I am writing this letter to show you that I know my stuff. Hoping you are well, I remain, your loving grandchild, Julian Kipnis. Regards to Uncle Louis." It's not hard to imagine the grandparents saving this letter, so endearing for its combination of formality ("Julian Kipnis") and slang ("knowing his stuff"), and the report of his good health. Julian was their only grandchild for twenty years, until I was born in 1941.

When the results of the bar exam are published in the *New York Times* on January 5, 1931—"1,104 Students Pass Bar Examinations and 1,137 Others Fail"—Louis gives his address as Macombs Road.

If Julian in the year 2000 brought me to my father in the year 1924, I need to push still further back in time to unlock the mystery not only of the relationship between them but of my father's relationship to his family of origin, the shadow family from whom Julian, my sister, and I had inherited the dunams outside Jerusalem.

My father's one story about growing up on the Lower East Side was an anecdote interrupted by his own tears and my mother's embarrassment at his public display of emotion: "I used to go to Hebrew School on roller skates," my father started to tell me one evening at dinner over Chinese food on the Upper West Side, when I tried to get him to talk about his past. My father on roller skates was almost as hard to imagine as my father as my mother's lover, or really, not to be ridiculously Oedipal, doing anything physical at all. Just to see my father behind the steering wheel of a car was to witness a body out of place. The only activity that ever seemed natural to my father was watering plants, at which he excelled; also, pleating the *New York Times* in neatly folded vertical columns on the subway, a skill no longer of much value for the growing population of online readers, and one I've never quite mastered.

My father looked pleased, if weepy, as he recalled his youthful daring. I waited, curious about this revelation. But before he could continue, my mother intervened. "Lou, pull yourself together," she said sharply, in a tone that turned the lone syllable of my father's name into an attack weapon. My father wiped his reddened eyes with the big white handkerchief he always carried and calmly finished the mu shu pork.

Is it any wonder I was starved for stories?

4. The Photograph from Kishinev

Rise and go to the town of the killings and you'll come to the yards
and with your eyes and your own hand feel the fence
and on the trees and on the stones and plaster of the walls
the congealed blood and hardened brains of the dead.

| Hayim Nahman Bialik, "City of the Killings"

What I believed as a child: we came from Russia. Russia, a vast, faraway, almost mythical kingdom ruled by cruel Czars, was filled with mean peasants, who lived in the forest with wolves, and even meaner Cossacks, who, when they weren't riding horses, or maybe *while* they were riding horses, specialized in something called pogroms. Basically, Russia was a place one left, if one was a Jew, as soon as possible. The fairy tale–like simplicity of this geography and its inhabitants did not include a longing to return. No one ever talked about going back there, wherever "there" actually was.

From Russia. But where? Where didn't matter. It was over there. So why did they come? Because of pogroms. What's a pogrom? Growing up on the Upper West Side of Manhattan in the 1940s, I imagined a pogrom as something like Halloween, a holiday we dreaded in our neighborhood because it meant being chased home by roving gangs of kids with stone-filled socks. We had few visual references for violence, unless you count *Bambi*, my first movie. Bambi running through the burning forest, me running out of our local movie theater, my mother chasing behind me. The Riverside, at the corner of Ninety-Sixth Street and Broadway, long gone, along with its twin, the Riviera.

So what's a pogrom? Motl, the young boy whose tale of emigration fills the pages of Sholem Aleichem's *The Adventures of Motl the Cantor's Son*, tries to get an explanation from another boy his age, Kopl, aboard the ship.

Kopl says to me, "You don't know what a pogrom is? Then you're just a little baby! Nowadays pogroms happen everywhere. A pogrom starts from nothing, but once it starts, it lasts three days."

"What is it?" I say. "A fair?"

"Some fair! They shatter windows! They smash furniture! They rip pillows! Feathers fly like snow!"

"What for?"

"What for?! Because! A pogrom isn't just on houses. They destroy shops! They throw the merchandise out onto the streets, they break everything up, scatter everything, pour kerosene over it all, and set it on fire."

"Go on! Really?"

"Do you think I'm making it up? Afterward, when there's nothing left to wreck, they go from house to house with axes, irons rods, and sticks while the police follow behind. They sing and whistle and shout, 'Hey fellows, let's beat up the Jews!' And they beat and kill and murder, stab with knives."

"Who?"

"What do you mean who? Jews!"

"Why?"

"What a question! It's a pogrom!"

"And if it's a pogrom—what of it?"

"Pogrom" comes from a word in Russian meaning to wreak havoc, to demolish violently. Although etymologically the word does not designate Jews as a pogrom's specific target, it has been associated with anti-Jewish violence since the late nineteenth century, when Jews were widely held responsible for the assassination of Tsar Alexander II. "Pogrom" served as a shorthand whose brevity nonetheless encapsulated the logic behind the giant exodus from Eastern Europe, even if some emigrants were also inspired by less tragic urgencies. "Pogrom" has become one of those umbrella words that shelters a collection of meanings, not least the complex motives for leaving one's country of origin.

"Pogrom," as a word, perhaps makes the most sense as the opposite of home.

For a long time, Kishinev and pogrom were linked in my mind, though I cannot retrieve the moment when I first made the association, or thought maybe that's where in Russia we were from. There was, I think, something suggestive in the repeating, overlapping syllables of Kip/Kish nis/inev that unconsciously intertwined the name, our name, about which I was always acutely aware, and that place. Internationally reported and then monumentalized by the great Hebrew poet Hayim Nahman Bialik's "City of the Killings," the Kishinev pogrom of 1903 radically changed the destiny of Jews in Russia and the wider world. When, in my late-life foray into my family's Jewish history, I began, from the evidence of this photograph, to piece together the story of the Kipnis family, I grandly attached Bialik's poetic narrative to my lineage as the crucial link in the memorial chain.

Once I made the Bialik connection, I started finding references in unexpected places—in Proust's *Remembrance of Things Past*, where one of the characters at a dinner conversation links the

Dreyfus affair and the Kishinev massacre, and in *Speak, Memory*, where Nabokov recalls his father's "celebrated article 'The Blood Bath of Kishinev'" as an instance of his father's acts of "antidespotic politics." It may seem a strange pleasure, but I enjoy seeing in literature the traces of the event that tie me to the geography of my past.

The portrait of my grandmother, grandfather, and my father's older brother, Sam, was taken in a photographer's studio in Kishinev sometime around 1903. Beneath the image is inscribed the name of the photography studio, F. Varshavsky, Kishinev. My idea about the date of this photograph is based upon the approximate age of the boy, who was born somewhere in Russia in 1897, and the time of departure for America of my great-grandmother and two of her adult children, who left a few months after the pogrom.

The act of sitting for a formal family portrait was something of a tradition in families on the verge of emigration, almost a sign of farewell. Possibly, my great-grandmother wanted a memento of those who remained behind—her oldest son and only grandson. Is this imminent family separation why the threesome looks so lost, stiffly posed on straight-backed chairs that branch out behind them like instruments of torture? But maybe they were just not happy to have their picture taken, or they felt intimidated by the photographer and his equipment. It's hard to know.

I stare back at this family, these foreigners of another time, another place, and try to fathom the nature of our connection. I note, remembering my mother's story, my grandfather's elegant ankle-high boots. But I'm riveted by the point of contact between the boy and his father: the slightly terrified six-year-old folding his tiny hand over his father's fist. By contrast, my grandmother seems self-contained in her own space, her hands clasped in her lap, indifferent to the needs of the boy who might have been trying to reach her through the layers of her skirt with his other hand.

Three years later, they leave Kishinev for New York.

Here is my one scrap of family lore about the trio's life in Russia, passed on to me by my cousin Sarah, for whom "Grandpa" is the boy Sam: "Grandpa told us that when he was young the Cossacks would come to their town and give the children a ride. At that point they were very friendly. His dad [my grandfather] had a tobacco store, and I guess they were people of means. The very same men who gave them rides came through the town, killing and looting. He used to say they came in the front door and he and his family fled through the back. Of course, they lost everything but what they could carry."

What did they carry?

For one thing, they carried this photograph.

According to the ship's manifest, a long rectangular sheet of paper lined and divided into ruled columns, my grandparents and their son boarded the ss *Potsdam* from Rotterdam. They are numbers nineteen, twenty, and twenty-one on this page, which contains the names of thirty fellow travelers in steerage (large steamships might have held 1,500 to 2,000 immigrants in steerage). I try to place the people of the photograph, my grandfather with his stiff white collar, tie, and three-piece suit; my grandmother in her beautifully laundered shirtwaist and long full skirt; and their neatly groomed and newly shorn little son, huddled with the others in steerage.

All the entries on the manifest, twenty-two categories in all, are recorded by hand and signed for by an immigration officer at the port of arrival. Of the passengers listed on this page, six were designated as of "Hebrew" origin ("Race or People," category nine, added in 1899). The other passengers were either Croatian or Hungarian. All the Hebrew passengers came from Russia. My relatives were the only ones whose last permanent residence (category ten) was Kishinev. Rafael was thirty-one, Sheyndel thirty-four, Shulem eight—or at least that's how the names and ages appeared on the manifest. (A few months later, on my father's birth certificate at the Lying-In Hospital of New York, Rafael is two years older, and Sheyndel/Sheindel is "Shingle.") Rafael gave his occupation as bookkeeper; all three of them could read and write. I pour over these documents, line by line, hunting for details that will help me re-create their history, fill in the empty spaces on what I'm calling my spline, the map of my vast ignorance. I know, for starters, what they are not: paupers, insane, felons (category seventeen); polygamists (category eighteen); anarchists (nineteen).

Not all the Motl stories treat the passage and the reasons for departure from Eastern Europe satirically. In "Mazel Tov, We're in America," Yom Kippur falls during the long journey and the passengers from first and second class descend into steerage to share the holiday: "And now they are wanderers, chased and driven like sheep to the slaughter, packed tightly together so that it's hard to catch their breath. Even the dressed-up passengers from first and second class" succumb to the emotion—to the painful acknowledgment of all they had left behind: "They are reminding themselves that just a year ago each of them was in his home, in his synagogue, at his proper place in his usual pew, prayer book in hand, listening to his cantor and choirboys."

The pogrom is the opposite of home.

On April 4, 1906, my grandparents were headed for my great-grandfather Chaim's residence, at 96 Allen Street. By then, the emigrants had become immigrants.

My father was born on December 19, 1906. Although I can't be sure of the date, my choices for the scene of conception are all limited to cramped spaces lacking privacy: if not on board ship, in steerage, on a berth—surrounded by filthy, seasick passengers—then in one of the jam-packed boardinghouses for emigrants that had sprung up in the port cities of the big steamship lines, on the road of more than one thousand miles from Kishinev to Rotterdam, at one of the many stops along the way. Or finally arrived in New York, in the tenement, crowded with an already established family of four or five on Allen Street, immediately upon arrival. The first evening of Passover fell a few days after their arrival in New York. Was my father conceived after the weeklong journey in anticipation of the holiday? The holiday that marked the anniversary of the major pogrom and so many others, the holiday marking exodus, leaving home, finding freedom?

The answer belongs to one of the many stories that were never passed on.

Five years after arriving in New York, my grandfather received his Certificate of Naturalization. The original copy of this certificate is the only official document from my grandparents' immigration preserved in the drawer. My grandfather became a citizen when he was thirty-seven; he was five feet five inches, white, of fair complexion; his eyes were blue and his hair brown; and he had no distinguishing marks. His wife by then, Sadie, was forty-one; his son Samuel, fourteen; and his son Louis, five. They all lived at 141 Stanton Street on the Lower East Side, not far from 96 Allen Street.

But if I knew more from these documents than what I had begun with (his blue eyes perhaps explained my green ones), there was something that continued to elude me. Born in Russia, yes, but *where*? I might never have known more about their birthplace than this, this mythical Russia, if I hadn't discovered the existence of an archive in lower Manhattan containing the "Petition for Naturalization," also known as "first papers." All I had to do was call.

Given a choice in the matter of requests, I always prefer the impersonality of e-mail. Every phone call designed to obtain information requires elaborate emotional preparation on my part, and I tend to delay for strangely long intervals: as much as I might want to find what I'm looking for, I also want to postpone the disappointment of not finding. But inevitably, at some point, ashamed by my procrastination, I propel myself into action. That's what happened the day I telephoned the offices of NARA—the National Archives and Records Administration—at 201 Varick Street. The person I needed was Bruce, but Bruce was on a lunch break. When Bruce finally came on the line, he asked me to wait while he went to look up the volume indicated on the Certificate of Naturalization. Of course I would wait. I had expected that Bruce (I never learned his last name) would tell me to put my request in writing. Thus far, except for Internet searches, all government documents I had been able to obtain had come through the mail, often after a period of weeks, even months. It seemed utterly implausible to me that I would be receiving this momentous information over the phone, as casually as if I were checking on an order from a Lands' End catalogue.

Bruce had trouble deciphering the handwriting on the papers and so began spelling out the name of my grandfather's birthplace. B, he began. B! It can't be B, it's K—Kishinev. I didn't utter the actual words, but my heart was directing, "Say K, not B." The photograph had convinced me that my grandparents were *from* Kishinev, and that was what I wanted to hear. Maybe B was really K. The next letter would tell. R. R? Now I knew that this precious information was going to arrive with a price. Bratzlow—Bratslav, as I was later to learn the town was spelled—Russia. Bruce then offered to read me the name of my grandmother's birthplace. This was unexpected bounty. I had not yet pondered my grandmother's origins. The first letter might be a T or a P then . . . maybe—aska, Russia. I asked for a copy of the petition.

Peschanka, Ukraine. In an e-mail exchange, volunteers from Jewishgen.org solved the riddle of the town's name. A friend, the historian Leo Spitzer, working with a detailed pre–World War I atlas of Eastern Europe, pinpointed the speck of a town for me,

44

sixty miles south of Bratslav and equidistant from it and Kishinev. For a few weeks I walked around stunned by my emergence from the glamorous vagueness of ancestral myth—Russia—and my insertion into the banal realities of historical factness, the concreteness of geographical DNA. *In the matter of the quest, location means everything.*

I already knew that my great-grandfather had listed Bratslav as his last place of permanent residence on the ship's manifest, so it was not astonishing that his son, my grandfather, was born there. But when did the little family get to Kishinev for their family portrait? Without the city as birthplace, could this still be my pogrom?

On the long sheets of first papers, there is stamped, in the blank space where the country to whom the petitioner—until naturalization—owes allegiance, the name NICHOLAS II EMPEROR OF ALL THE RUSSIAS. There is also a new location to insert into the narrative: July 21, 1906, Rafael was living at 279 East Fourth Street when he filed his "first papers," only three months after arriving. Now that I'm launched in my investigation, I scrutinize obsessively, with Talmudic attention, every available detail on the pages before me—both the boilerplate language of government documents and the handwritten particulars. A clerk has scrawled "Austria" and crossed it out to replace the signifier with "Russia"; family names are spelled in several different ways on the same page. I note the names and professions of the two witnesses to my grandfather's petition—Sam Rothenberg, Paper Dealer, and Nathan Beerman, Peddler, neighbors on the Lower East Side.

Appended to the petition to become an American citizen is my grandfather's application to change the spelling of his name from Rafael to Raphael. Compared to his wife's transformation from Sheindel to Sadie, the move from Rafael to Raphael is small and soundless, making for only a more American-looking spelling. But my grandfather decided to inscribe the desire for citizenship in the new appellation. I take the decision seriously, to the letter, seeing in the gesture a wish to seal the transformation in his autobiographical identity with a sign. Perhaps my mother's story about this grandfather, that he couldn't adjust to life in America, wasn't entirely true, at least not in his beginnings.

I return to the mysteries of the family group portrait with my new knowledge. The portrait was taken in 1906, I decide—not long after the arrival of my grandparents from Kishinev—in a photography studio on the Lower East Side, perhaps after my grandfather filed his first papers.

Who are they? The severe-looking woman to my great-grandfather Chaim's left is my great-grandmother Sore (later Sarah); the young woman standing behind my grandfather Rafael (perhaps already Raphael) and my great-grandfather Chaim (later Harry) is Zirl, his daughter, a twenty-two-year-old seamstress, according to the manifest. The boy with glasses is his son Itzvchok, an eighteen-year-old laborer (later Isaac, then Isador, and finally Isidor). I still haven't identified the tall, thin man between the brother and sister.

If the Kipnis clan felt elated at being reunited in America, you wouldn't know it from this picture. Their elbows press into each other, but on the whole, set against the implausible backdrop of a rococo forest with its filmy trees and potted palm in the corner, this strangely arranged family looks like a group of lonely monads, each enwrapped in solitude and even sadness. By 1906 images registered quickly enough for the sitters to smile, but the tradition of not smiling, well established in the nineteenth century, when photographic sessions were slower, may have persisted. Photographs have a way of hiding as much as they reveal.

Seated at opposite ends of the front row, the Kipnis wives are separated from each other by their husbands. My grandmother seems oblivious to the pressure of her little son's body as he leans into her, just as she had been in the Kishinev portrait. Meanwhile, her mother-in-law, Sore, receives her own son's comforting touch on her shoulder, his hand sticking out from the much-too-long sleeve of his jacket, borrowed for the occasion perhaps; she also feels the pressure, if not affection, of her husband's elbow against her. Gazing straight ahead, my grandmother further distinguishes herself from the family group by the fact that she alone holds an object in her hand, the purse, whose shiny surface draws my eye. Her index and third fingers catch the purse's chain and the pleated panel of her dress together. Wearing a dress that emphasizes her short torso and makes her arms appear strangely truncated, my grandmother, in a complicated maneuver, tries to keep the purse from falling as she pulls her dress down over her pregnant belly.

When I look at this photograph now I see the family constellation of the world that my father, the first Kipnis to be born in America, was about to enter.

5. The *Nudnik* and the Boss

The image of my father as a little Jewish kid skating to Hebrew school on the Lower East Side came back to me when I opened a manila envelope labeled in my father's writing "R.K. Letters in Hebrew" on one side and "Talmud Torah letters" on the other. The letters turned out to be lengthy documents, handwritten on long, lined, yellow sheets of legal paper, stapled together. They also turned out to have been written in Yiddish, not Hebrew, as I learned when I finally had them translated. My grandfather had marked the letters, which were pale but legible copies of the originals, with a hand stamp bearing his name, address, and telephone number. There were also a few letters addressed to my grandfather, which, judging from the names written in English on the masthead, seemed to belong to a brief flurry of correspondence between my grandfather and his colleagues on the board of directors of Talmud Torah Anshe Zitomir on East Fourth Street. Would my father and his father have saved these pages if they were just the minutes of a meeting of the board of directors?

With the correspondence, the grandfather who had died before I was born sprang to life: Raphael Hirsch Kipnis, a man whose entire legacy to me, as far as I knew, and one I had already pocketed, was a silver cigarette case engraved with his initials.

On January 21, 1929, Max Meyerson, the president of Talmud Torah Anshe Zitomir, an after-school program of religious education for children, writes to my grandfather Raphael Kipnis, "the Hon. Rec. Sec.," as he is listed on the masthead. Typed on letterhead stationery and composed in correct English, the president's letter addresses my grandfather as "Worthy Director"; clearly, the men enjoy their honorifics. Brief and to the point in his formal prose, Mr. Meyerson encloses tickets to the annual fundraising event to be held on March 12, 1929, at Maurice Schwartz's famous Yiddish Art Theatre, at Fourteenth Street and Fourth Avenue. The play being performed at the benefit was Sholem Aleichem's romantic comedy *Stempenyu, the Fiddler*, in rotation with *Tevye the Dairyman*. Mr. Meyerson urges my grandfather to accept the tickets—that is, to pay for them—and to encourage others to buy them, too. As president, he underlines the importance of the "annual entertainment" to the survival of their institution and the future of the Jewish boys and girls who attend the school.

In a personal handwritten postscript, David R. Zaslowsky, the principal of the Talmud Torah, admits that he knows that my grandfather will not be "too thrilled with boxes" but that he assumes that his response—because it's not *any* theater, but the Art Theatre, and "just because," as he puts it in Yiddish—will, despite his dislike, nonetheless be favorable. He adds that the enclosed tickets are for six boxes at $2.50 apiece, for a total of $15, and mentions, presumably as further incentive, that the boxes are on the same tier as that of Mr. I. Gilman, "the Hon. Pres. of the Talmud Torah."

Like many Sholem Aleichem stories, the discussion between the secretary and the principal turns on details and small domestic matters between husbands and wives; the worlds are never separate. Writing to his "beloved friend," my grandfather casts himself as a supplicant figure, subjected to his wife's will. His wife, "the boss"—he uses the English word in Yiddish—isn't happy with the seats. Why is this? My grandmother doesn't like box seats because they bring her too close to the boxes of the rich. She doesn't have the right clothes for her proximity to the well-heeled women attending the performance, she protests, and she doesn't have time to shop. So please, my good friend, obey my boss's orders and send orchestra seats. And not just any seats: no closer than the third row, no further back from the stage than sixth row center. The boss is specific. My grandfather encloses a check for $15, along with the original tickets. The boss will divorce him if he is unsuccessful in his efforts to obtain different seats.

Like one of Sholem Aleichem's talkative, letter-writing small businessmen, who belonged to a rapidly disappearing world, my grandfather was steeped in tradition but stepping gingerly into modernity, along with the railroad car, at the advent of the twentieth century. The formal man with the white stand-up collar and knotted black tie, waistcoat, and long jacket, who sweetly smiles in almost all the photographs I have seen, touches me by his storyteller's eagerness to please.

"Ordinarily, when the boss gives an order, one must obey. Therefore, I beseech you to act upon my boss's command," he implores. Was my grandmother really the boss in their household? Or was my grandfather just adopting the cliché of bossy wife and henpecked husband, already a staple of American culture by the 1920s? The joke goes on a little too long in the letter to feel either serious or truly funny. Perhaps there was no other way for Raphael to ask his friend for a favor without the embarrassment of asking directly. My grandfather seems to relish, even as he complains about, his role as his wife's messenger; she, through him, jointly signs the letter: "Raphael and his wife Sheyndel." I comb through this letter looking for clues to their marriage, to this couple in their early fifties, who by 1929 had been living in America for more than two decades.

"Women," my grandfather continues, introducing another anecdote about his wife, "women are something to be reckoned with." This story, my grandfather warns, must remain between the two men, not least because it concerns the president's wife, Mrs. Meyerson. If Sheyndel, as she remains in Yiddish, refuses to sit next to the rich, she certainly doesn't want to chat with them at the theater. Mrs. Meyerson meets Mrs. Kipnis at the theater. Mrs. Meyerson asks for news of my grandfather's parents, suggesting that they should all socialize sometime. My grandmother is skeptical about the woman's motives. "That's very nice of Mrs. Meyerson," she comments with a sniff, as if to say, "Why should she want such a relationship?" Then Raphael adds that his father "finally" died. The Meyersons, it seems, sent "a penny postcard" at the time, saying that they hadn't heard about the death. Mrs. Kipnis, annoyed, suggested that they send a postcard back to inform them of the news.

The story about my great-grandfather's death and the Meyersons' reaction to it seems to be a prelude to the real point of the narrative, a question from my grandmother about the Meyersons' finances. My grandfather tries to distance himself from the inquiry by telling his friend that he is quoting from the "text" (that's the word in Yiddish) of his wife's recital: "You probably know how much I care about these sorts of things," he writes, looking for a disclaimer. He then turns around and does his wife's bidding: What is the value of their company? In other words, how rich are the Meyersons, really? I confess that this is the kind of slightly baffling, roundabout story that if told by my parents would be followed by the comment, "You have to know Yiddish." And, not knowing Yiddish, I would shrug my assent. I still do.

Raphael in 1929 could have telephoned his good friend to discuss the matter of the tickets. But no, he decided to write—and to write in Yiddish: "Thanks to the ticket problem, and Mrs. Kipnis's annoyance, I have been given the opportunity to write you a few words in Yiddish. If you find my letter to be grammatically incorrect, please correct it yourself." Despite his faulty command of the language, Raphael was happy enough with the results of his composition to make and save a carbon copy.

The ticket problem, it turns out, was not so easily solved. The "beloved friend," the principal, answered Raphael a few weeks later. He replied, also by hand and, like my grandfather, dating his letter with the Torah portion, approving my grandfather's effort by referring to it as his "last very delightful modest and humorous letter." Writing on letterhead from the Talmud Torah, the principal addresses the business at hand (the tickets), reserving his response to the rest of the letter, he adds, for his leisure at home. My grandfather's plea on his wife's behalf has not worked. Writes Mr. Zaslowsky: "It is apparent that He who turns the world on its axis has reason for various explanatory exegesis that we, even through intervention, cannot actualize for you and Mrs. Kipnis." Short version: the seats cannot be changed.

Zaslowsky plans to write more fully at a later date. "I don't have the letter here as I put it away at home to cherish for many years to come," writes the principal of the Talmud Torah Anshe Zitomir to "Honorable, successful, admired, venerated colleague and esteemed teacher, Reb Refoyl H. Kipnis." He signs off, with regards to my grandmother and my father, as "Your devoted friend who would sacrifice his life for you." The two men indulge each other's talents as letter writers and play with the mix of levels that connect them: they note the Torah portion, they bless the respective families, and they self-consciously negotiate the gap between the sacred and the profane. They seem to write for the pleasure of it—even if the letters turn around the business of the Talmud Torah. The men also compete as to which is the better writer. "If only I could write as well as Mr. Z.," Raphael complains, "I would write to the papers—specifically to the *Tog.*"

Like Sunday painters, they are Sunday writers.

Two weeks later, Raphael, referring to himself as the "director of the Talmud Torah," dates his letter of Sunday, March 24, as the week of Purim. The holiday is inscribed in black ink, which stands out against the yellow of the carbon and its faded handwriting, and the date is given in the upper right-hand corner of the page both in Arabic numerals and in Hebrew. In this second letter there is no mention of the tickets, the theater performance, or even his wife, the boss. This seven-page handwritten letter, which revolves around a matter of some importance to the men's common enterprise—the possibility of their school merging with another, neighboring one—allows my grandfather to fool around with the friends' shared concerns. Purim is a holiday that authorizes, even mandates, drinking. Either my grandfather composed this letter under the influence, or he took advantage of the convention in order to experiment with self-expression, creating fictitious personae and different voices that would take him out of his daily life.

The experiment doesn't quite work. Raphael's not really a happy drunk or a successful fiction writer, but the letter's incoherence offers a clue to what it might have cost my grandfather to reinvent himself in America when he was well into his thirties. In the course of this ostensibly playful performance, my grandfather seems almost desperate to confide in his friend. Framing his effort as a search for relief, he "unburdens himself to whomever it may be," he states at the start. And in concluding, he uses the

expression twice more: "If only someone would lift this burden
from my heart and write a few endless words for me"; and again,
staging himself in the third-person character he invents in this
letter, "It is already not willingly that I put everything down on
paper that your friend Mr. K. unburdened from his heart." It's as
though he can't quite help himself.

What attracts him to the metaphor of the burden? What is
weighing him down? And why, in 1929, is he now living in New
Jersey? My grandfather lived on the Lower East Side from 1906,
when he arrived at Ellis Island, to at least 1926, when he signed
the documents for the property in Palestine at the Stanton Street
address. From 1909 to 1916 his occupation in the New York City
directory is listed as "agent" or "manufacturer's agent" at 119
Ludlow. Whenever a document—the ship's manifest, his World
War I army registration card, my father's birth certificate—lists an
occupation, my grandfather identifies himself as "bookkeeper." In
1920 the city directory lists Raphael as secretary of the "People's
Bag and Paper Co. Inc."; and in 1922–23 he surfaces with the
business address of 362 Fifth Avenue, "Manhattan Commercial
Corporation," directly across the street from the former B. Altman
department store, the still beautiful Renaissance Revival building
that now houses the CUNY Graduate Center, where I teach, at 365
Fifth Avenue between Thirty-Fourth and Thirty-Fifth streets. Unlike
365, my workplace, 362 is an undistinguished office building,
currently hovering over a Duane Reade. Its blank façade leaves
me clueless as to Raphael's whereabouts in the late 1920s. I can
only follow the paper trail—the steps of a man whose destiny
seemed quite literally bound up with paper. In the 1930 federal
census for North Bergen, Raphael's occupation is again listed as
"bookkeeper" and the industry as "Paper Boxes."

I often visited my maternal grandfather at his tailor's shop, one flight up on West Thirty-Fifth Street in the heart of the Garment District. Grandpa Miller cut—when we were children in the 1940s, he made our winter coats—but Harry sewed. I doubt that I ever knew Harry's last name. I'm not sure he ever looked up from the machine. Did he even speak English? There is a bronze sculpture of a tailor, "The Garment Worker," bent over his sewing machine on Seventh (now Fashion) Avenue and Thirty-Ninth Street that tourists like to capture with their cameras. The tailor is an aging Jewish man (he is wearing a skull cap), whose spine is fixed in a permanent curve. He looks exactly like Harry, though perhaps somewhat younger. Adjacent to the sculpture stands a gigantic stainless-steel needle, poised at an angle, piercing the hole of an equally super-sized button, in case anyone missed the symbolism.

Two blocks east of my grandfather's shop is the building on Fifth Avenue where Raphael Kipnis worked for a few years in the 1920s; it's around the corner from the Empire State Building now, but in the twenties and early thirties, that southwest corner was the site of the Waldorf-Astoria Hotel. Recently, I started imagining an encounter between the two men, but I have no way to make it happen, except in my imagination, especially since the years don't quite match up, and I don't in fact know how long my grandfather had his shop in that specific location. Still, it's tempting to make them meet. What difference did those few blocks make to those two men, my two grandfathers, as they discussed (in what language?) the match between their American-born children?

"Now I live in a small town in New Jersey," my grandfather writes to his friend Mr. Z. in 1929, without explaining why he has left the Lower East Side and his beloved Talmud Torah. But the bond remains alive. In rehearsing the dilemmas of their Talmud Torah to Mr. Z., Raphael apologizes for his long letter and his lack of talent as a writer: "Oh well, if it were writing checks, I would be better at it." And here, almost in closing, comes the refrain about the burden: "If only someone would lift this burden from my heart and write a few endless words for me." It's difficult to know how to take the sadness—or false modesty—of Raphael's sigh: "I am full of heartache." Maybe keeping the books for others is itself a burden of boredom.

Let me say it. With its proliferating cast of characters and impenetrable internal references, this *Purimspiel* is hard to follow. The jokes don't quite work, including one originally in a mixture of Hebrew, Russian, and Yiddish that defeated the translators. In addition to the Mr. A., B., and C. interlocutors, my grandfather has created Mr. Whomever and an imaginary Mr. K., his alter ego, who visits the letter writer in New Jersey. If that weren't confusing enough, the presiding persona of the Purim pastiche is an unidentified character called "your friend the *Nudnik*." The *Nudnik* appears at the very beginning and end of the letter—at the beginning as Mr. Z.'s friend Mr. K., and at the end, before the signature, as Mr. Whomever: "What do you think of your friend the *Nudnik*?" As if to say, "So what do you think of my fancy accomplishment here?" "A *nudnik*," explains Leo Rosten in *The Joys of Yiddish*, "is not just a nuisance; to merit the status of *nudnik*, a nuisance must be a most persistent, talkative, obnoxious, indomitable, and indefatigable nag."

A self-identified *nudnik*, of course, is no *nudnik* at all.

Purim gave my grandfather Raphael a chance to play at being the *nudnik*, to take the time to share with his dear friend his concerns about their threatened Talmud Torah and their disagreement about its future. Raphael opposes the conversion of their school into, as he puts it with a dose of righteous indignation, "a center that would produce baseball Jews and swimming pool Jews." Raphael seems genuinely outraged by a potential future merger: "I cannot understand this. Maybe this is because I am always on the side of the Jew. But our friend Mr. Z. also says we should unite!" I'm moved by the *nudnik*'s passion for his school's mission, the community it has created, and its friendships, even its contentious committee meetings. "Oh wouldn't I love to be in Talmud Torah," my grandfather writes to Mr. Z., almost with a sigh of longing. "Meeting or no meeting, I would love to spend an hour with you over a drink, but there is no time."

In December 1929, two months after Black Tuesday, my grandfather writes a letter in English to one Mr. Sam Beerman in Pittsburgh. Perhaps Sam was the brother of Nathan Beerman, the peddler who witnessed my grandfather's first papers decades earlier. The note was saved as a typed original on my grandfather's personal notepaper: R. H. Kipnis, 5533 Hudson Boulevard. "Am interested to know if the proposition we took up several years ago still interests you," Raphael writes to his friend. "I have a proposition which you might like. Kindly communicate with me at once." I can't tell whether the letter was answered or even sent.

When David Linetsky, the president of Zitomer Talmud Torah Darchei Noam at Avenue B and Eighth Street, writes to my grandmother on the occasion of Raphael's death, he encloses a resolution from the board, in English, praising her husband's dedication: "He worked most incessantly for the perpetuation of Judaism, and improvement of the religious training of Jewish boys and girls." His friend Mr. Z. is still the principal, but the new address suggests that my grandfather's resistance to the combining of the two Talmud Torahs did not prevail, since the two institutions have merged their mastheads. I don't know whether the swimming pool Raphael scorned was built.

"What do you think of your friend the *Nudnik?*"

I asked my translators what they could guess about my grandfather from his Yiddish. His quotations in Hebrew were correct, they said, and ventured that in Russia he had had an old-fashioned *cheder* education not unlike the one he was helping foster in New York. His penmanship was not beautiful, they said, and was often hard to read. He sounds like a businessman, not an intellectual. That seemed fair enough for a man accustomed to keeping books and writing checks for other people, but perhaps they missed the note of longing I thought I heard in my grandfather's voice, the longing to be someone and somewhere else. I recognize that longing in myself, the desire from childhood to be elsewhere; I wish I had heard that voice when I was growing up, desperately wanting to be someone I wasn't.

Without the letters I would never have encountered the *nudnik* and the boss, the couple that produced my father. Without the letters I would never have known that when my father married the boss, the model had preceded him. Was my father a secret *nudnik*, too, then? I'm forced to ask myself the question.

I doubt that my father was able to read his father's letters (after all, he thought they were in Hebrew, not in Yiddish), but like me, he couldn't throw them away. If he was the second saver, I am the third.

Of all the objects that have given me this story, the cigarette case most resembles the kind of object that would, in the ordinary course of things, be handed down—a family heirloom. The delicately curved case is inscribed with my grandfather's initials, RHK. The

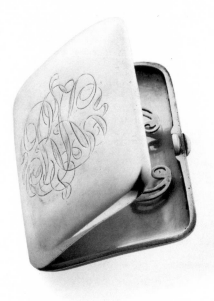

silvermark is inscribed in tiny numbers on the inner edge of the case; inside, the clips that once held hand-rolled Russian cigarettes are now just elegant squiggles. I described my grandfather's cigarette case not long after the inheritance of the dunams sent me to meet my cousins in Memphis. The silver object generated the epilogue to my last book, which is, not least, a meditation on how our autobiographical stories, ideas of who we might be, bind us to others. I wrote about the cigarette case then, in the first flush of astonishment caused by discovering this family whose existence had been known to me by name only. I did not imagine then that I would continue, I want to say, polishing. Not just literally but as a metaphor, or better, a metonymy, a figure of speech that expresses the connection between things, and that helps me gather up and mend the fragile ties to the vanished side of the family, a story to stand in, even make up, for all the stories that were never told. I know so much more now than when I started that I had to return for another round.

The chain of inheritance.

As Sarah tells it, Sam's wife Rose (RK) gave Raphael's cigarette case to Julian for his wife Ruth (also RK), who smoked at the time. Later (how? when?) the cigarette case was transferred (by Julian?) to my father. I had coveted the slender silver object even after I had stopped my compulsive smoking. The smoking, I figured, made the object mine, even though my sister, Ronna Hope, inherited my grandfather's initials, RHK. Standing in front of the chain-link fence on the Lower East Side, my grandfather seems to be holding the silver object between his thumb and index finger, in the palm of his right hand. I can trace with my fingers the slight indentation where his thumb must have grasped the case. In almost all the family snapshots, the men pose with cigarette in hand. In almost all the pictures of me until I was forty, like the generations of Kipnis men who preceded me, I had a cigarette between my fingers. When I started smoking in the 1960s, I thought I was cool; I had no idea I was following in a family tradition.

Sam died of lung cancer in 1976; Julian died of lung cancer in 2002. The cigarette case is not just a memento but a memento mori, a reminder of a family's very bad habit.

It's difficult not to fear that I'm next in line.

6. Family Trees

It wasn't hard to see that here on this faded sheet of ruled paper was the beginning of a family tree—a Kipnis genealogy. My roots.

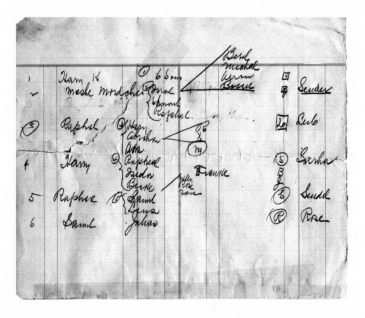

When I do tree pose in yoga, I wobble as I stand on one foot, trying to find my balance. Root to rise, the teacher instructs. Do I imagine that by extension, when I assume the pose metaphorically and discover how I am connected to past generations, I will feel more complete, more balanced as I look toward the future? Why this sudden need for roots?

In the euphoric days of seventies feminism, I rejected roots, family, and my father's name as hopelessly patriarchal. Here I am back, decades later, reclaiming my father's name but having problems with the tree. And not any tree, but the cartoon tree of generational imaginations, the great oak with its single, massive trunk; its roots deeply set in the ground; its branches reaching to the sky. The phallic order of knowledge, as we liked to say then.

I was struggling over the language of what sounded like a return to the roots I had repudiated when, on a recent trip to Hawaii, I was introduced to a kind of tree I had never seen, a tree that seemed made entirely of roots. The Banyan tree throws out aerial roots, which first emerge laterally from the original trunk; then the new branches hang, until they reach the ground. From there they solidify to form another pseudotrunk, in a kind of side-by-side cloning. As luck would have it, a cluster of these trees was located next to a municipal archive in Honolulu, and I was seduced by the idea of creating a new tree from the materials of the already standing one, a new archive self-consciously created from the top down. I'd find roots by the very gesture of looking for them, creating the outline of a family narrative that I've had to invent.

In the absence of stories passed down, of ties maintained, of documents preserved, I've embarked on a project of rerooting, rerouting, reimagining this family that until recently was almost entirely lost to me. Re-creating this family, however, is not an attempt to establish bonds where none existed. It's more a matter of putting these tiny shoots of information, these bits of archival DNA, into the history from which they were excised through silence, and imagining what might have happened if they had been put into words.

Unfortunately, I did not recognize any of the names inscribed on the list, beyond that of my great-grandfather, my grandfather, my father, my uncle, and his son, my cousin Julian. Above these family members, and in the columns to the right of the page, were ancestral names with alternately biblical and Yiddish echoes: Abraham, Moishe Mordecai, Sender, and Schmul. In lonely splendor, at the top of the list, presided Harry K. It all began with Harry K. and his six sons. But who was this Harry K., who presumably began life as Chaim?

I was mystified by the long line of Kipnis generations whose existence I had never begun to fathom. I concluded from other examples of his handwriting that my grandfather was the author of this primitive genealogy. Raphael was a bookkeeper by profession, so perhaps he had torn a page from an old ledger, which is what the ruled lines and columns suggested.

I knew from other documents in the drawer that my great-grandfather Chaim died in 1928 and Raphael in 1934, and that Sam's son Julian was born in 1921. So perhaps, after the birth of his first grandchild, Raphael decided to look back through the generations and place himself in the chain, in a fifth generation of sons. The only sure thing was that the tree began before March 1934. Perhaps my grandfather consulted with his father, Chaim, who shared the name Harry K. with the first Kipnis ancestor.

The page was folded in half. Inside I found a second attempt at a genealogy, this time in my father's hand. My father went beyond his father's draft, adding many names, which he numbered, and sketching a tree with branches.

Did father and son sit down together and compare notes? Or did my father, after his father's death, find the piece of paper, turn it over, and continue on his own, alone with the puzzle of descent? My parents married in 1936. Since my mother's name is

not on the chart, I take that date as the outer limit of this second composition.

In 1990, when I first uncovered this piece of paper in the drawer and guessed that the tree had been composed by my grandfather, I did not yet know that his father, my great-grandfather, had lived part of his life in New York. But no sooner do I write those words than I realize that this is not quite true either. When my father died in 1989, my sister and I found the letter from his brother in Arizona, written on the occasion of their mother's death. In it Sam recalls a conversation with their father, on the occasion of their grandfather's funeral. I could at that point have thought: that would be my great-grandfather. But, strange as it now seems to me, now that this history has become a full-on obsession, I did not think then about the generations beyond my grandfather. I did not stop for a moment to realize that I had a great-grandfather who had immigrated to this country. I simply filed the letter away, along with the other objects and correspondence. I did not wonder about the relationship between my father and this great-grandfather, whom he had never mentioned.

Even stranger was my failure, when I first contemplated the hodge-podge of my father's papers, to connect the cardboard photograph of mystery family members with the ancestors named on the trees and mentioned in my uncle's letter. When my father died, the pressures of the immediate future (the funeral, the emptying of the apartment, the will, the business of becoming his executor) were what mattered. Something important was coming to a close—my life as a daughter—and that absorbed all of my emotional attention.

More than twenty years later, having scrutinized the contents of the drawer and compulsively inventoried my family archive, not only can I connect my father to his grandfather, but I can also put faces from the photographs on the numbered slots of the family tree. For the first time, I'm able to glimpse the lineaments of a story that my father did not pass on to us but that he must surely have possessed, not least because many of the cast of Kipnis characters—ancestral ghosts to me—had to have been known to him. These missing people haunt me. Harry K., my grandfather begins, had six sons. It did not seem to have occurred to him to wonder about the mother of those sons; perhaps he did not know her name. Harry is also number 1 on my father's tree, but the space corresponding to number 2 is blank, and my father has placed a check mark next to the number, as if the absence of a female name in a quest for origins had caught his notice. Who, what woman, was at the beginning of the other side of this family?

I remained baffled by the trees, which pointed to a forest of relatives I had no way of tracing, until Fran Bailey, the amateur Kipnis genealogist I had met early in my quest, created a new tree from the information my father's numbered chronology contained. For the first time I could literally see the generations as they stacked up, reaching back into what seemed to be the eighteenth century. I had no hope of reaching a generation beyond that of my great-grandparents, except to learn their names from my great-grandfather's death certificates. But immigration records made it relatively easy to track my grandfather's brother Isidor because he registered for the World War I draft and because he changed only his first name, keeping the same initial. Isidor must have remained in my father's world for a while. I caught a glimpse of him in the home movie of my parents' wedding in 1936; and in a snapshot in the drawer, he is nattily dressed, smoking a cigar and reading the newspaper, looking much the same. There was also a separate studio portrait of Isidor taken not long after the family portrait, where I can see that he, too, had the kinky hair I inherited. I succeeded in having a telephone conversation with his eighty-year-old daughter-in-law, who was living in Charleston, South Carolina. From Dorothy Kipnis I learned that Isidor had been in the first class of the College of Pharmacy at Columbia University and had owned a pharmacy in Brooklyn as late as 1930.

But I could discover nothing comparable about his sister, Zirl—my grandfather Raphael's sister and my great-aunt—whose formal portrait was also collected in the drawer of family photographs. In the 1906 family portrait, she bridges the generations, gently reaching down to her father and her brother. I became obsessed with finding this great-aunt, whom I resembled, I thought, because of her pale, narrow face and her dark, puffy hair.

Fran zeroed in on a blank, marked with the initial "B.," next to a Louis, one row from the bottom of the resurrected tree. Since she had located Isidor on my grandfather's line and since she knew that Harry/Chaim was the father of three, Fran reasoned that B. had to be Beckie (from my father's compilation), a.k.a. Zirl, who had married Louis. The next leap was to figure out how "Zirl" (a Yiddish variant of the biblical "Sarah") had become "Beckie." "I agree it's a big name change," Fran wrote, "but her mother's name was Sarah; and maybe if Rebecca was her middle name, she used that to avoid confusion."

Warren Platt, the helpful expert I had met at the New York Public Library, picked up the trail. In an archive for brides, he found not one but two Beckie Kipnises—one of whom turned out to be ours. The marriage certificate revealed that my great-aunt Beckie Kipnes (Sarah and Beckie had used that spelling for several years) had wed Louis Jacknes (later Jacknis) on February 13, 1907. All the details fit: Beckie's parents were Harris and Shora (by now I was accustomed to the myriad spellings of first and family names on any number of documents, from birth to death). She was born in Russia and, at the time of her marriage, lived at 192½ Delancey Street, with my father's family. My father would then have been a one-year-old. "A match!" Fran writes in the subject line of her e-mail.

With the details from the marriage certificate, I located the naturalization petitions for Beckie and her husband, and I learned that Zirl had been born in Podolsk, a town west of Bratslav and now on the border separating Ukraine and Moldova. The couple had three children, the youngest of whom, Rose, had in 1938 signed the death certificate of my great-grandmother, her grandmother, with whom she shared an address on Madison Street on the Lower East Side.

Was this the end of the line?

Rose died in 2000, the year I began this research.

Looking back, after the exhilaration of the hunt, I'm still staggered to see that I can attach myself to a history that reaches more than six generations into the past, including branches of relatives I had never dreamt existed. For in her thoroughness, Fran had also included other branches of the Kipnis tree on separate sheets.

She was surprised that I had never heard of them. "One thing puzzles me," she wrote. "The descendants of Israel and Esther Kipnis lived in Brooklyn and the NYC area. I can't help but wonder why you never heard about them, or met any of them." That is the question that I've not been able to answer: Why had I never heard about any of them? Closer to home, why had I never heard of Beckie and Isidor, my great-aunt and great-uncle, who had also lived in New York?

I'm left with that mystery, that silence, but my father's tendency to hoard outwitted his failure to tell his family's story. I don't think he would be sorry that I've tried to rescue that story from the drawer, from the archive of forgotten lives and of people he once loved, who came from a world they had left behind. That lost world was, for him, the first of his family to be born in America, a treasure of possible knowledge, inherited but never fully known, collected, and stored in a drawer full of abandoned memories.

I like to think of my tree-making as a posthumous collaboration, picking up where my father and grandfather had left off, connecting the names, numbers, and faces to an imagined community of ancestors, including, at the beginning, the no-name ancestress I have decided to call Sarah.

7. Suicide in Argentina

The more I learned, the more I worried. Why had my father never mentioned the existence of his grandparents, or of his aunt and uncle, who had emigrated with them? Why did I never meet his brother? I could not answer those questions, but I could not stop wrestling with them either. After all, my father had left me enough clues to fill in at least the outlines of the immigrant story he had never shared or acknowledged. Working through the inventory of the drawer over the years, I could not resist the thought that my ancestors had been affected by the horrors of the Kishinev pogrom, and I used this to explain to myself the peculiar history of Kipnis estrangements, the disappearance of so many family members—people who lived in New York and whom I could have known. Maybe the trauma of the pogrom had even filtered down through the generations to produce me and my Russian melancholy, my less glamorous American depression. It was impossible to know, of course, but equally impossible not to consider.

For a long time I had wondered about a letter in a thin, pale-blue airmail envelope, frayed around the edges and missing a stamp. The letter was addressed jointly to my father's brother, Mr. S. Kipnis, and to my grandmother Sadie in North Bergen, New Jersey. My grandmother's name, spelled "Sade," was written off to the side, twice, one above the other on the envelope; the

family name had also been added below, a second time, spelled Kipnes. On the envelope, the town's name was Hispanicized, Norte-Bergen, and located across the river in New-York, America Norte. Amazingly, the letter had reached its destination.

The return address only compounded the enigma. It began with the notation Asociacion Israelita, which was followed on the next line by a surname I didn't recognize. The rest of the return address read Entre-Rios 1471, Rosario (St. Fe). Who was the sender of this letter written in Yiddish? Why had my grandmother, and then presumably my father, saved it? I had no idea, nor did I suspect then how crucial the stories of my uncle and my grandmother would turn out to be in solving the mystery of the vanished Kipnis line.

Almost twenty years after my father's death, I finally had the letter translated. Why was I keeping documents in my possession that I couldn't read? Maybe the letter would flesh out my portfolio of silenced stories and disappeared relatives.

On the last page of the letter, in a convoluted turn of Yiddish *politesse*, the writer identifies herself as my grandmother's sister: "Please extend the most friendly and dearest of greetings to your loving and dear parents, they should live a long life, and extend to your loving mother that she has a sister that was given as a present to her because no one expected her to survive this ordeal. My friendliest greetings to your loving brother"—and she refers to my father, her nephew, by his Yiddish name.

The letter, two double-sided, yellowed pages covered in neat blue handwriting, is a blow-by-blow account of an operation: "From my belly, they took out such troubles and they left it in the hospital, so they could study it. Ten doctors were present at the operation, including students." My great-aunt's letter is one long narrative of pain relieved as it is relived—a celebration of survival, thanks to God's intervention. Survival but not good health, not so fast: "And don't think that I can eat everything. They also need to warm my liver with electricity. I need lots of warmth, because now we have winter, in a word, everything is upside down." The letter is postmarked June 29. The year is not visible, but from the address I know the letter had to have been written between 1929, when my grandparents moved from the Lower East Side to the little town across the river in New Jersey, and April 1933, when they moved to Brooklyn, the era of the Talmud Torah correspondence. Sam was by then living in the Bronx with his little family, but the Argentina relatives did not seem aware of that development.

I confess that I was at first disappointed, though not truly surprised, that Dvorah Weisman was not a Yiddish Mme. de Sévigné. My great-aunt's prose was animated by a cosmic *oy* of the kind my parents mocked. We were quite deliberately not *oy vey* Jews. Yet here was the joy of Yiddish in a dithyramb of suffering. The letter brought not just the gift of language but the discovery of another point on the spline of the family's Diaspora—a third sister, who had settled in Argentina. And then, some greater sense, however allusive, of what these people—my people—had left behind, probably in the wake of World War I: "It has been already eight years that I don't feel well, and hardly a day goes by that I shouldn't feel pain, but everything seemed like good times compared to what we lived through in Russia. We didn't pay attention to the pain and didn't make a fuss over it, therefore, when we came to the golden land, Argentina, I was in big trouble, I constantly fell apart, and a couple of times, I was so sick, that no one believed I'll live through it."

Dvorah's comparison of her bodily pain to the difficulty of life in Russia enchanted me even as it provided a poignant measure of the suffering endured in the world they had left behind. In my hunger for palpable traces of my missing family, I loved hearing, I confess, the litany of her misery and its crude language—my great-aunt's sense of triumph over those who thought she had a belly full of schmaltz, not serious trouble that had to be removed. Here was a glimpse of all I would never know directly but could only guess at through the accident of a single saved letter. I was especially taken by the Yiddish lessons the translator gave me when she included the occasional idiom that defied translation. And "everything helped like a bean tied to the wall," Dvorah commented, describing the useless remedies applied by the doctors before she was finally taken to a Jewish hospital in Buenos Aires for surgery. It's not hard to see why the letter was saved, with its vivid description of suffering and triumph, near-death, emergence into life—Dvorah adds "Khaye" ("life," in Hebrew) to her name—a Passover story, as she dates the narrative.

On the back of the envelope, someone (my grandmother?) penciled a short list in Yiddish—blanket, nightgown, dress—and jotted down numbers that appear to be an addition of expenses.

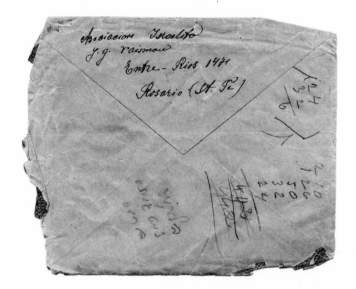

Were these items to be sent to Argentina? Preparations for a trip? Perhaps the letter circulated for a while, to be shared with friends and relatives, until finally set aside for safekeeping.

Sometime after the translation of the letter from Argentina, and looking for something else, I stumbled upon the reply from my father's cousin in Canada about the people in the family portrait I could not identify, a letter that summarized the arc of Dvorah's life but whose content I had failed to absorb.

The roots-seeker's blindness: I wasn't looking for her, so I didn't see her.

Sadie was my mother's (Sarah) sister. There was another sister Dvorah who was the youngest of the females; she emigrated with her husband and their two daughters to South America. I think only one daughter remained—the parents died, the older daughter was unhappy in her marriage and committed suicide: leaving a small boy. We have lost track of the remaining daughter.

I know nothing about where exactly they came from—but I do know that Sadie's father was the overseer of an estate belonging to some wealthy Russian man. As for Raphael's family, we know nothing about them.

My mother took me and my sister Fredi to visit our grandparents once when we were very young children—too young to remember very much about the visit. It was the one and only time we saw them.

We, my parents and my three sisters and I, emigrated to Canada in 1921. My mother corresponded with her parents and family but they never saw each other again. However, Sadie visited with our family many times and my mother went to New York once, I believe.

They never saw each other again. On my second reading, I was riveted by this geography of loss. Three sisters. A suicide. This was Chekhov territory. How could I have missed this? I suddenly remembered a photograph, with Yiddish writing on the back, of a family that felt both strange and familiar. Maybe this was Dvorah; she looked something like my grandmother, with the same square, unhappy face of the Kishinev photograph.

The greeting, in the neat Yiddish script I now imagine I recognize, reads: "Dear Sister! Don't be surprised that I have aged so. It is still me and it is all for the good considering that I am constantly ill. And the *naches* we are experiencing from our daughter demonstrates I am made of iron. So this is why I look so ugly." The third sister, Dvorah, whose face reflects the unhappiness of the message, holds a little boy, presumably her grandson, on her lap. I'm guessing that the young woman standing behind the bench is the boy's mother, the *naches*-giving daughter. This young woman resembles her Canadian cousin to a striking degree. The translators have left the word *naches*—the mixture of pleasure and pride that come typically from children—untranslated. It's one of the dozen or so Yiddish words that I know and that the translators figured were part of my limited linguistic inheritance.

But how can *naches* mean that Dvorah is made of iron and, at the same time, that she is ugly? My translators said they understood *naches* as maternal sarcasm: the daughter's troubles (*tsuris*, the opposite of *naches*) were causing the suffering and the ugly face. This daughter was unhappy in her marriage. Dvorah would assume, in sending the photo, that her sister, her family in New York, were aware of these problems.

Sometime around the miraculous recovery described in the letter, but probably close to the time the snapshot was taken, Dvorah's daughter, "unhappy in her marriage," "committed suicide, leaving a small boy." Not long after I connected the letters and the photograph, I came across a wedding picture I had puzzled over when I first saw it, the portrait of a couple, unknown to me, taken in Rosario. On the back was a greeting in Yiddish: "Dear brother-in-law, sister, and Kipnis family! Enclosed is Etyushele's wedding picture. Please let us know that you've received it. The second picture is for Sam and his family." By then I knew who the sender had to be.

I'm not really surprised that my father never told me the story. But I can't help wishing I had known. I wonder whether my father recalled his cousin's fate when I was suicidal in my twenties, also unhappy in my marriage. Perhaps he feared that, like bad marriages, suicide ran in the family, his family, and worried that I took after my grandmother's line.

8. Wolf and Virgin

My father had come to the party with a date; my mother had tagged along with her older sister. At twenty-five my father had recently graduated from Brooklyn Law School. At eighteen my mother was still a student at Hunter College, a French major. Their encounter was a *coup de foudre*, love at first sight. They were of an age to marry, but obstacles in their individual family situations blocked the progress of the marriage plot on both sides: my father's father died unexpectedly, and my mother had to wait for her older sister to marry (or at least get engaged) first. Of course, they held hands and kissed.

That was it. They waited. And look how happily their marriage turned out.

Those must have been some kisses.

The tale of their courtship, as it came down to my sister and me, was romantic but also didactic. It was told as part of a lesson about sex education in the 1950s, when we were adolescents. My mother remained a virgin until they married, despite the fact that my father was, my mother always said in telling the story, a wolf. No amount of eye-rolling or other signs of incredulity on our part (four years?) would shake their story.

I had grown up wondering whether it would happen to me that way, the love-at-first-sight part. I believed the taming of the wolf, even half-believed the myth of my virginal mom, but until I had plunged into the mystery of my father's lost family, I had not thought (and why would I have wondered?) about how, in coming together, this couple had also set in motion the disappearing act that resulted in the missing Kipnises.

My evidence resided in a packet of letters neatly tied up in a back corner of my mother's dresser. During the summer of 1934, from late July through mid-August, my mother and father exchanged over thirty letters, the only correspondence they seemed to have preserved; perhaps it was the only time they were separated. I had discovered the letters in the underwear drawer after my father's death. I had found them amusing, touching, but no more than an artifact of sentimental value, something like my letters home from summer camp, which my mother had also saved. Proof that we had all once been young.

The first of the letters is a note with the date inscribed in Roman numerals, October 17, 1932. Attached to the note, on heavy cream-colored stock edged with a blue border (the envelope is edged in blue as well), is a small black-and-white snapshot of my father with a male friend; on the back is written "Waldemere 1931" (Waldemere was a popular hotel in the Catskills). My father had added an arrow pointing to himself, "always thinking of something to eat," before signing off with a measure of mock formality, "With kindest personal regards, I am Lou." Lou seems confident enough of his charms not only to send the silly photo but also to fool around with my mother's name on the envelope; as if to inscribe the sheer pleasure of capture, he makes the three "M's" of Miss Molly Miller resemble a slanted roof. This "Molly Miller"—it takes him another letter to master the correct spelling of her name, Mollie—lived with her family in an apartment on 105th Street and West End Avenue, about ten blocks north of where I currently live, and one block from where I grew up, 105th Street and Riverside Drive.

Among the letters is a small newspaper clipping glued to a piece of blue-colored paper, the date typed, "Dec. 18, 1932," the day before my father's twenty-sixth birthday: "Court Frees Women in Relief Bureau Row; Rebukes Their Counsel, Orders Every One Out" reads the headline in the *New York Times*. My father had been defending three women and one man "for disorderly conduct at the home relief bureau" in Brooklyn. The reporter notes: "A large group of alleged Communists were in the court room, but there was no disorder." This is the first trace I have of my father's career and public life. One of my parents, or both, had decided they had embarked on a story worth keeping.

December 31, 1932, my mother turns nineteen. My father hand delivers a tiny note containing his business card, on which he has penned birthday greetings; perhaps the card came with flowers. On the back on the envelope, in pencil, my mother has written, "New Year's Eve at Little Ritz Club" and the date, "12/31/32."

On January 24, 1933, in the second of the four short letters that precede the summer correspondence, my father sends my mother directions to the Sixth Magistrates Court in Brooklyn, where he will appear between 9:30 and 10 a.m. The entirety of the note's contents is composed of the itinerary by subway that my mother should follow—the Elevated line, he underlines. He signs the note, two months before FDR's inauguration, "New Deal" Lou. On the back of his letter, my mother has added in pencil her own directions to the departure point noted in Lou's instructions. The couple is recto and verso of the same 7 x 10 piece of office stationery (heavy but translucent stock), pen and pencil. Her handwriting never changed; his faltered only at the end of his life, when the micrographia of Parkinson's disease overtook the elegant penmanship that had once been his.

March 13, 1933. My father has walked off with a copy of Descartes' writings (no less—I just have to say that: no less) belonging to my mother. They have disagreed about the relative merits of their different translations. My father (who has never studied French) wants the last word on the subject. "In a day or so I send you my thoughts which are terribly scattered since I read this chapter." And then, as he signs off: "Am I dizzy? You're telling me!" My father has met his match; I wish I knew which chapter had set his head spinning.

April 7, 1933. The third billet-doux is again composed on letterhead stationery: Louis Kipnis, Counsellor at Law, with an address at 305 Broadway, New York. (I miss the elegance of life before zip codes, when New York was enough.) My father writes to give my mother a new home address, "different from that which I gave you on my card." The new address is "496 Autumn Ave, Brooklyn NY." My father doesn't explain why he is moving to Brooklyn (with his parents, which he doesn't say). But something has happened: "So far," he observes in a two-line paragraph, "I have not been terribly affected by the turn of recent events."

The note continues, enigmatically: "It appears that with normal luck we ought to make a go of our new venture. It may involve some sacrifice on my part for a short time after which fewer demands on my time will be required. Of course I am not begrudging these demands." I conclude that the "we" includes his parents, since they are moving together to the new address, but what events have led my grandparents to leave North Bergen? Is my grandfather pursuing his dream of a paper business in the heart of the Depression?

"So-o-o-oh, until I see you," my father signs off. "I remain (as ever?)" he coyly questions with a tag to the formal closure, "Your 'great lover.'" It's unseemly, I admit, to want to know what it meant for my father to call himself a great lover between quotation marks in April 1933, when he played big bad wolf to my mother's maidenly virgin.

My father squires my mother and her sister (my mother is on my father's left) in a snapshot dated June 1933, soon after my mother's graduation from Hunter, hatted, suited, and on the stroll, arm in arm. The stork on the store's logo suggests children's clothing. I make out a word ending in "iddies." "Middies," blouses for women and children? Or maybe it's "kiddies." It's hard to see into the window. It's hard to resist the metaphor: wanting to see into the window of these days, shadowed by the striped awning.

Why do I care so much about who these people were before I knew them? Because the effects of the couple they formed in this courtship never ceased seeping into our lives as children.

Maybe the primal scene is the romance, not the sex.

In March 1934 my grandfather died at the new address on Autumn Avenue in Brooklyn.

At the end of July 1934, my father accompanied his mother from New York to Montreal, Canada, by train, where her sister and her family lived, for a one-week vacation. "There was a reunion of families," my father writes about his arrival in Canada with his mother. "There was a very brief crying period and then we got in the spirit of things." The fact of my grandfather's death passes quickly in the circumlocution.

In her first letter to my father in Canada, my mother, in full heroine mode, reviews the sequence of emotions that receiving his "prompt letter" produces: "The desire to see you made me sentimental, this sentiment almost causing me to write you a weepy letter. But stop! Cease! Halt! says I, no Miller ever wrote a weepy letter." The Millers had an idea about themselves that the Kipnises lacked. It was that idea that, in the end, winnowed the already diminishing Kipnis ranks.

For lovers in epistolary novels separated from each other's presence, every minute of every day counts, but my father takes his accountability literally. His love letters provide the organization of his day, even documenting his tourist activities with physical evidence. One letter from the trip north includes a map of the

Montreal area clipped from a local newspaper that he asks my mother to save for him.

Along with the map comes an enumerated list of my father's daily schedule from 10 a.m. to 10 p.m. and his first impressions of Montreal. He is struck by the "tremendous illuminated cross" atop Mount Royal, "visible for miles around except when its view is impaired by other crosses"; notes the religious demographics of the region—"We are in Montreal, the home of the monks, nuns and Canucks"; and reads the signs announcing prohibitions and fines that, to him, seem typically French—"Defense du"—"garbage, smoking, spitting." My father fancies himself a linguist, but he omits the accent on the prohibition (*défense*) and gets the preposition wrong (*de* is what it should be), I note pedantically; I know, I know, it's tacky to notice, but I can't help myself, once a French teacher. But I'm not the only one to track errors. My mother corrects my father's spelling in one letter and then adds a mistake of her own, calling him "mon chère," marking the term of affection in the feminine. Reading these letters I see the structure of hypercorrection that would flourish in our family's competitive style. Even now, I can barely resist correcting the spelling of the dead.

"My poor sweet," my mother replies. Now that she has graduated from college, she is working for an insurance agent (no teaching jobs, despite her training), enjoying the "casualty work," and taking dictation. She's good at it, she boasts, fast. She writes, "It certainly must be hard for you to travel about and see all those crosses. Anti-semitic [the lower case is hers] as I am, I'm afraid it would even irk me." Both my mother and father came from Orthodox Jewish families; both made a great show of Jewishness when we were growing up, insisting on the importance of the identification. I'm intrigued to see my mother joke about herself as being "anti-semitic" and even more by the turn she makes with it, dismissing the crosses: "Don't waste all that passion in denouncing that most annoying practice, save a little of it for a well deserving sinner, such as me."

In most of the letter my mother speculates about the date of my father's return to New York, but she manages to remember the purpose of the journey: "How is your mother getting along? I hope she's having a nice time." My mother is never effusive when it comes to her future mother-in-law.

"Dootsey-Bo-Bo" is the name my father has earned as an "honorary Frenchman." She's "Tootie Toot." They send kisses. "I too have this thing called nostalgia," he admits. "However it is for a person and not a place. I give you only one guess as to whom I mean." The New York summer is hot. The Millers are moving around the corner to a building where the landlord is offering concessions. Six rooms and three baths. "Public Enemy No. 1 JD was killed coming out of a movie." It's the thirties, after all, though I wonder whether John Dillinger makes her think about my father's brother—his connection to Dutch Schultz. One of Mollie's brothers is getting married. The family has been discussing the plans. My mother jumps the gun: "Sweet, I think we'll elope" and later pens in a caveat ("if ever") . . . "an afterthought," she adds.

I unfold and refold these small, neat envelopes, the pages covered with regular, even lines of handwriting. They both enclose ephemera from their daily lives, especially my father, who conscientiously documents his travels with tiny clippings, ticket stubs, a bus transfer, a weight card (missing from the envelope) showing that he has gained a pound—and a report that he has been washing his socks. Sock washing in a love letter. Only now, after a long marriage of my own, do I begin to understand this.

Jewish/not Jewish. The binary organizes their world. My father goes to court with a cousin: "From the spectators' benches the first sight that greets the eye after seeing the judge is a tremendous crucifix (it looks like an ivory carving) on an oak panel. The only consolation is that Christ isn't bleeding from the spikes driven into his extremities." My father listens to "French, English, and Jewish lawyers," goes to a Jewish restaurant (finds it like Jewish restaurants in New York). But what difference does the difference make? He concludes his letter, posted July 26, with a flash of Yiddish: "*Alzo* Mrs. Bloom—*ich ver tzuchmaltzen* and close with love and kisses."

Mrs. Bloom was the upstairs neighbor with whom Molly Goldberg chatted in their Bronx tenement on *The Goldbergs*, the wildly popular radio program of the period, with Jews and their trials of assimilation center stage. "Yoo-hoo, Mrs. Bloo-oom!" Molly would shout out the window to the airshaft. It's not hard to guess that my mother Mollie, whose family always lived on the Upper West Side, would both recognize and want to distance herself from that world. What was my father doing with the reference? So, Mrs. Bloom, *ich ver tzuchmaltzen*, I'm melting. Melting from the heat, of which he has just complained? Or melting in desire—in Yiddish, the language both theirs and no longer theirs. I'm guessing that the melting was a pun that Lou expected his Mollie to get.

She's water to his schmaltz: "Rudy Vallee is singing his head off, but right now listening to soft music turns me into a waterspout." I try to picture my mother weeping over my father's one-week absence, but the overlay of the exasperated mother and tough woman she became in my eyes has blotted out the sentimental girl forever.

Then, in my mother's letter also postmarked July 26, for the first time the outside world briefly and abruptly makes a cameo:

"Incidentally, now that you're away, deprived of your pacifistic influences, it looks as if dear old Europe is going to have a nice old-fashioned war. Tonight's radio reports were a little more optimistic. Whatever happens, darling, I hope we won't get into it, because most of all it means you and Dave [her older brother]. But let's worry about that when we come to it." On July 25 the Austrian chancellor Dollfuss was assassinated, and political disturbances followed.

"Oodles & packs & carloads & busloads of kisses."

"Your one & only (I hope) Mollie."

I love this kissy, silly mother. Where did she go? "Have you been true to your love?" she asks, ending with a flurry of postscripts, pleading for reassurance: "P.S. Honey, as a special favor will you please tear stain a couple of pages, so that I'll be convinced that you really miss me. P.P.S. Honey, I love's you. P.P.P.S. Honey, it's hot as blazes, but still I miss you. P.P.P.P.S. Honey does you miss me? P.P.P.P.P.S. Honey, does you still love me?" The folksy play with incorrect grammar doesn't disguise an anxiety that continues for several days, as she waits for my father to write back and break a silence that she finds intolerable.

Despite her anxiety, my mother is not afraid to launch a full-on attack on my father's manner: "How do you manage to acquire the air of impersonality in your letters? You always manage to detach yourself from any description or narration that you give. You make me feel, for the most part, when I receive a letter from you, that my emotion and sensations which I describe and write to you about are an expression of adolescence, infantilicity (?) or a little silly. Please don't take this as a rebuke, but let me know whether you feel that way about it." By the time I knew my mother, rebuke was her primary mode of communication.

Reading the letters, I want to shout at them like the narrator in Delmore Schwartz's beautiful and terrible story "In Dreams Begin Responsibilities." In Schwartz's famous tale, the young narrator dreams, "as if I were in a motion picture," that he sees his parents courting before he is born and tries to warn them not to marry: "Don't do it," he cries out, as the couple verges on marriage. "It's not too late to change your minds, both of you." I want to warn my mother, don't do it, he will never tell you how he feels. This "air of impersonality" is not just an affectation on the part of the man you are in love with; it is his emotional style, the man himself. That capacity for detachment will not change, and it will drive you crazy. I know—it drove me crazy, too.

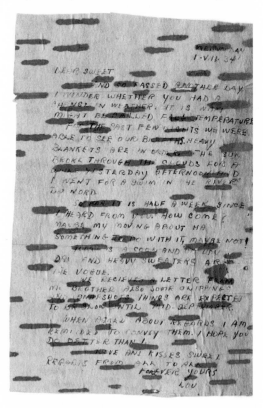

My father's next two letters are written on birch bark, as if to authenticate his commitment to the daily report. The weather—they both comment on the weather—it's summertime and, except for the mountains, it's hot. But the weather will remain the staple of my father's correspondence to us as children and the bedrock of his vision of the world, recorded in his date book and travel diaries, for the rest of his life. He has received a letter from his brother in Arizona, with "some clippings and snapshots." He notes, "Things are expected to go slow until mid-September."

The snapshots, pictures of Sam and his wife starting their new life in the restaurant business, came in twos—one with Yiddish writing on the back for their mother, one in English for him. The lives of the brothers diverge but are still in the early moments of the separation, connected by the thread of familial bonds. The letter home is sent to mother and brother. With the death of Raphael in March and the departure of Sam in August 1934, the Kipnis family shrinks down to the dyad of my father and his mother.

My father gets points for the birch bark—"it certainly was a novel experience"—but the effort entailed doesn't prevent my mother from typing a long and coruscating complaint about my father's epistolary skills: "I must tell you that you are not a very satisfactory correspondent." Details ensue about the failures in my father's performance, including the timing of his letters. I must tell you, she said to me once, as she lay dying from cancer, your father was not a very satisfactory lover. The dissatisfaction must have provided its own kind of emotional fuel.

My mother is desperate for my father to tell her what his plans are. Doesn't he realize that she is leaving on vacation? Will they see each other? Doesn't he care? "I suppose this letter sounds mean and nasty," she writes, winding down, "but I can't help it, because that's just the way I feel." "That's just the way I feel," the theme song of our family's life, the anthem of righteous anger. "Good Lord," she explodes in her long, long letter, changing the tone in a flash from cloying dependency to active aggression, "don't you even miss me? You don't so much as mention it. You're one of those annoyingly self-sufficient people." Finally, though, my father surrenders and delivers the much sought declaration: "The fact that I fail to pen lyrical protestations of love and anxiety does not mean that you aren't always in my mind and thoughts. I miss you in all ways. Physically (decently) mentally spiritually and truly. You wrote that you do too which makes me truly happy."

Naturally, I want to know about "decently." They are only in year two of the four-year moratorium. But I'm equally entranced by "truly happy," which I think my father was, with my mother and in his life, though the expression of it was not part of his emotional vocabulary.

August 13. The trip to Canada is at last over and my father is visiting with my mother's parents in their new apartment. My mother has taken a one-week vacation in the Catskills with her sister, Fay. Lou has dinner with the Millers and returns home to his mother's apartment to sleep. For the first and only time in the summer exchange, my father reflects on his mother's situation: "By jiminy, my mother certainly is a heroine and good soldier doing as well as she does. I don't see you for a few weeks at a time or like tonight for one night and I feel a void. I can imagine her feelings." *By jiminy*. It would be hard to find a more incongruous—less Jewish—expression to introduce the subject of his mother's widowhood. But if empathy for his mother leads him to an atypical expression of feeling for my mother, he makes no connection—here or elsewhere—to what the loss of his father might have meant to him.

My mother writes from Hotel Brickman in South Fallsburg, New York: "It's a real Jewish hotel, but of a better class. The meals are good, even though they are a bit filling." The entertainment surprises: "They put on a show yesterday that was excellent. They feature a fairy. He gives me the willies, yet he is fascinating." The two sisters have dinner with the fairy, who turns out to be a married man: "He's doing Mae West, Joan Crawford, and others tonight." Despite the tennis, the swimming, the ping-pong, the slot machines, and the flattering fairy (he told the sisters they were pretty), the "wootie-toot" misses her honorary Frenchman, even though this time she's the one who's gone away: "Honey I love you I love you I love you I love you that's all that I can say."

The last letter from Hotel Brickman reprises the Jewish theme: "Well, mine love (incidentally, I've developed a Jewish accent associating with these Hebes. You anti-Semite)." Earlier, when my father was ranting about the crosses that studded the landscape around Montreal, my mother called herself an anti-Semite. Here, she makes my father the anti-Semite, but what does it mean to banter with those words? Both are intensely aware of the sliver of time that separates them from their immigrant parents—and their accents. (Many years later, when my mother applied for a teaching certificate in New York City, she was initially rejected because of her "New York" accent—dentalization and sounding the final "g"—those traces of another, déclassé speech pattern that Hunter College, and before that Hunter High School, worked so hard to erase in its girls, along with poor posture. My mother wrote infuriated letters to the Board of Education in protest.)

My mother doesn't want to be one of those "Hebes" cavorting in the Catskills, but she wants someone—my father—with whom to be Jewish (you still had to marry one), "Hebes" together, only different. In 1934 America, while the war in Europe is still remote, it's possible to joke *en famille* about anti-Semitism, to imagine oneself another, fancier kind of Jew. American-born children of ambitious Yiddish-speaking immigrants, Mollie and Lou form a new couple who will never return to the Catskills, which, by the time I know them, they disdain.

"I hope you go up to my house sometimes," my mother writes from her week's vacation. "Lord help you if I find out that you don't." But he does: "I am at your house now and have just had supper. I have been talking with your mother until now when I took 'time out' to write and she to prepare for your father. Al [the younger of my mother's two older brothers] is at his usual Monday night [bridge] game." At home in Mollie's absence, Lou joins her family's rituals, as the newly widowed Sadie Kipnis sits alone in the Bronx.

My mother occasionally expressed a kind of limited sympathy for her mother that was also a form of condescension: What could she have in common with a woman who cooked and cleaned for four children and numerous relatives, including her own illiterate, Yiddish-speaking, mother? "Little children, little problems; big children, big problems," was the inherited wisdom that my mother evoked, ritualistically, with an imitation of her mother's singsong accent. My grandmother, whenever she saw me, quoted my infant cries for food, as they accompanied percussive banging on the tray of the high chair: "Meat, meat." A demanding, carnivorous child.

My mother's sense of separateness, of distance—what could her immigrant mother possibly know?—is palpable in her surprise at my grandmother's reaction to a tantrum my mother confesses to my father, faced with the news that his return to the city has been delayed: "I was so mad when I got your letter this morning that I decided not to even answer it. Well, my mother just told me a thing or two or three. I didn't think she had it in her." I didn't think she had it in her. I took up that same position in relation to my mother. What could she possibly know about me? A genealogy of misprision.

In addition to the packet of letters from the summer of 1934 are a small number of communications between the couple, telegrams and birthday cards, from earlier and later, the last one dated December 1936, as the courtship mode closes. After that date, although it will be another five years before they become parents, the traces of their exchange vanish (except for news of my first tooth, announced by telegram to my father's office). Writing this, I've begun to wonder whether their many years without children explains the distinctness of the image my parents fashioned together and projected to the world: they were first and foremost the couple they had constructed. What to do, then, with the children?

This story of that young couple in love, which I can easily map onto the grid of Manhattan streets that I've walked hundreds if not thousands of times, feels so close. And yet no matter how close I can get to the spot—stop, linger there, at that very address where my weepy mother read the letters from my father who was melting—the people they were that hot summer forever escape me. But their letters have become mine, and reading them I'm melting, too.

part 2

Saving the Name

9. The Mayor of South Tucson

I do not remember asking my father why we had never met his brother. It was one of those facts of family life that in childhood appear so implacably obvious as to require no explanation. But as I wandered through the labyrinth of my father's papers, I could not help feeling that some noir secret had kept the brothers apart. After all, my father traveled to California on business. He could have made a stop in Arizona and taken us with him, if he had wanted to. In that first summer after leaving New York, Sam had written to his brother, proudly displaying his early success in Arizona.

What happened between them after the snapshots of 1934?

I type my uncle's name into the computer. I'm stalling. I'm still in the dark about this man. Somehow, he feels more foreign to me than my dead, immigrant grandfather, and more elusive. Beyond my cousin's stories about his father's past that I had heard when I went to Memphis, I cannot recall a single anecdote about Sam, an adjective to describe him. To my astonishment, in the nano-second of Internet delivery, three items pop up: an article from the *Tucson Weekly* from August 2000 about the history of South Tucson, a listing from the Southwest Jewish Archives, and a reference to an archive in the South Georgia Regional Library Services (this last Samuel Kipnis turns out not to be my uncle but a man of almost the same age and from another of Sholem Aleichem's villages). The *Tucson Weekly* reporter, David Devine, recounts the heroic history of the little town's efforts to incorporate—"Today's Breakaway Burgs Could Learn from the Early Tribulations of South Tucson"—and mentions the part played by Mayor Sam Kipnis in the struggle, even quoting him. The tiny band of citizens' impassioned bid for autonomy, beginning in 1937, devolved into a bitter, decades-long resistance to the no-less-intractable determination of Tucson politicians to annex the towns around it.

In the familiar pattern of double take that both impeded and rescued my quest from the beginning, I recalled seeing a clipping about Sam and South Tucson in a folder along with several letters from him to my father. I had noticed the skinny column of newsprint in the course of my postmortem inventory, but I had not yet decided that I wanted to know more. There it still was, slipped inside a folder marked "Arizona" in my father's hand. "South Tucson Elects Kipnis." This was no small item: "In a brief but momentous session," the *Arizona Daily Star* reports on June 3, 1937, "the new South Tucson town council elected Sam R. Kipnis mayor." Now, of course, I was burning to uncover everything I could about the public life of Sam R. Kipnis, the first elected mayor of South Tucson.

South Tucson in the 1930s measured four blocks wide by one mile long and had one only paved street. Small as it was, the majority of the town's inhabitants did not want their little community (fewer than one thousand people) taken over by Tucson, the big city that wanted room to grow. The residents of South Tucson preferred to control their own destiny, even if it meant running the town with volunteer firemen—and doing without city water. For a desert town, the danger of fire and the difficulty of getting access to water were not trivial preoccupations.

In the *Smoke Signal*, another local publication, Devine high-lights my uncle's starring role in the David and Goliath saga and captures his public personality: "Mayor Kipnis, as was his fashion, bluntly stated the obvious: 'One too many municipalities is trying to control building permits in South Tucson.'" I studied the pamphlet with the attention I used to lavish on eighteenth-century French journals in the stacks of Butler Library, when I was a graduate student at Columbia University. It felt strange to be introduced to my uncle through the archive of a history I knew nothing about and whose icons were cacti against a desert landscape.

My uncle the mayor was unwavering in his beliefs: "Defeated but still defiant, Mayor Kipnis aimed a parting shot at the members of the Tucson Council before leaving the meeting." Soon after these public shows of independence, however, my uncle "fell on his political sword and resigned from the Council." Summarizing the mayor's all-too-brief career, the journalist Devine revisits the *Arizona Daily Star*'s pro-Tucson coverage of the controversy: "Kipnis's resignation removed from the official ranks of the town a man who at the same time was one of its most enthusiastic citizens and the center of the many storms that have assailed it since its incorporation almost nineteen months ago." Although the mayor's arguments did not prevail, and several punishing setbacks ensued, the little town ultimately resisted annexation, thus giving Sam Kipnis something like local-hero status in the annals of the region.

I marveled at the portrait of a man—my uncle—falling on his political sword, as he resigned from office. How had this man, new to Arizona in 1934, so quickly become a center of attention, not to mention storms? How had he acquired a sword to fall on and heights to fall from? True, the town was minuscule, but something had to have made it possible for him to jump into the fray with a certain élan. South Tucson was populated by people who had come from elsewhere. By the time Sam arrived in its precincts, the square mile of South Tucson was already a place where not too many questions were asked about credentials and pedigree. That atmosphere seemed to inspire him. He was even responsible for the much commented upon acquisition of the town's lone, fully equipped fire truck, whose bells and whistles brought his celebrity to new heights.

In one of his stories, Sholem Aleichem refers to a character as "world-famous in Boiberick," the imaginary name given to Boyarka, a small town in Southwest Russia. In South Tucson, I started to think, Sam had migrated from one Southwest to another, one Boiberick to another, with his years in New York as a temporary big city hiatus. Maybe the small-town scale of his village came back to him in memory.

Now that I've found my uncle in his public persona, I try to weave together these new sources of history with my cousin's matter-of-fact assertion that during Prohibition Sam had worked for the "Dutchman." How can I connect the dots between that Sam and this local celebrity in South Tucson politics—rewind the reel? For one thing, how did the nice Jewish boy my uncle presumably once was end up hanging out with gangsters in the first place? According to Sarah, who had grown up in Tucson in the 1950s, Sam's wife's sister, Ray, was a manicurist in New York, and "some of her clientele were Mafia." Sarah explained, "Sam was out of work so Ray asked if they would give him a job. They did." Reading Sarah's words now, I feel the same conflicted mix of incredulity and belief that jolted me when the information first appeared on my computer screen. What exactly was Sam's job? I asked, reaching for a casual tone. "It was collecting money from all the businesses," she replied. Sometimes my uncle would take Julian along with him. I play the movie in my head, scenes framed in memory from endless representations of little Mafiosi going from store to store in rundown neighborhoods, picking up envelopes bulging with cash. This would have been in the late twenties and early thirties, when Dutch Schultz was making headlines.

For more details, I flesh out Sarah's picture with E. L. Doctorow's best-selling novel *Billy Bathgate*, about a young man's apprenticeship to Dutch Schultz. I borrow the young hero's changing fortunes—Billy's starting salary ($250 as a streetwise, uneducated boy) working for the Dutchman—to imagine my uncle's adventure. I revise my picture of Sam, now, like Billy, stuffing the bills he collected into small brown paper bags, not envelopes as in the Italian mafia movies. I figure that, like Billy, Sam got something of an education in numbers, watching the men in the backrooms calculate the percentages on horse races. Sam "kept a count as he turned in the money," Sarah explains when I share my novel-reading information with her. "He was not the one who kept all the books." Oh, I think, impressed by the distinction that makes the fantastic story more concrete. "He was a small fish," she adds later.

At the Cotton Club, where Sam delivered the money, father and son must have chatted with "the crime family," as Sarah described the network of major and minor players. But she dismissed her father's footnote to the narrative that the gangster was his godfather. Maybe, she concedes, as a child, excited by the Dutchman's powerful aura, Julian had embellished the relationship in his mind and created the fantasy of paternal protection. I press Sarah to tell me what she makes of this legacy. "As to the Mafia," she assures me, "Sam told the story as did Dad. Ray has told it as she was there. It never bothered me. I thought it was interesting and being a kid, it was cool. I used to tell anyone who was mean to me to watch out."

Cool. Sarah's just two years younger than I am; we grew up in the same rigid fifties culture. But my mother's relenting social aspirations and my father's love affair with the law meant that our home style was always the opposite of cool. That my father failed to tell this family story consolidates my suspicion that something unseemly like the gangster connection kept the brothers apart.

I stare at Sam, handsome and brooding in a World War I army uniform, a wool khaki tunic with a short standing collar and flap pockets. He's wearing the signature Montana Peaked hat, with its crisp broad brim and distinctive indentations, slightly tilted on his shorn head at a rakish angle. The photo is set in an oval studio background and printed on a piece of thin cardboard designed to serve as a postcard—a postcard, in this case, never addressed. (Invented in 1907 these were called "real photo postcards" and were instantly popular.) This one never made it into the mail, unless it arrived in an envelope. The remainder of tape around the edges of the card suggests it had once been glued into an album or scrapbook, but whose? A child seems to have scribbled on the photograph. There is no date. Perhaps Julian as a little boy played with the photograph one day, imagining his own future as a soldier.

Thanks to the Freedom of Information Act, I learn that Sam served in the 1st Co. 152nd Depot Brigade, from May 8, 1918, to May 17, 1919. If I've succeeded in matching the uniform in the photograph to the military records, I've still no idea what my uncle actually did during the war or where he served. The number on the sleeve of his jacket suggests that he was a supply sergeant.

Any scrap feeds my hunger for knowledge. So despite not having the information on Sam's military activities during that one year, I am overjoyed—after many attempts to persuade the "archives technicians" at the National Personnel Records Center in St. Louis that my uncle had served and that there must be *some* record of that service—to receive, months after I had given up, the discharge papers of Samuel R. Kipnis. The text of the disbursement states that "all men whose names appear on this payroll are entitled to Sixty Dollars ($60.00) bonus under Act of Feb. 24, 1919 War Dep't." Next to my uncle's name is the amount of $161.13. I can't tell whether that included the bonus.

With each query, the machinery of discovery sets in motion a predictable pattern of joy or disappointment, sometimes both at once. Each outcome temporarily halts the process, as I question my obsession. Sometimes I feel overwhelmed by the amount of time and the intensity of emotion I've invested in the search. Sometimes I'm made ridiculous in my own eyes by the excitement that any piece of information, however small, brings me.

You have to—I have to—resist the fascination of collecting information for its own sake, just because I can. I learn, for instance, by clicking on Camp Upton, where my uncle was "separated" from the army, that Irving Berlin spent his year there as a draftee writing a musical, including the song "Oh! How I Hate to Get Up in the Morning." Maybe Sam met Irving before he was demobilized.

The embarrassment of riches that flows from the resources of the Internet finds a counterpart in the embarrassment of engaging in the quest itself. How many hours and how much money are you willing to set aside in search of lost ancestors? Unless you are independently wealthy or retired (or both), you must develop a regimen of self-control, a system of checks and balances, otherwise you run the risk—I did—of losing the plot, forgetting what you were trying to discover and why. If you are also a writer, you must ask yourself why anyone else should care about what you find, and admit that they might not.

When I found myself wondering whether my uncle had met Irving Berlin at Camp Upton, I knew I had gone too far.

But then, how far is far enough? I could not seem to give up on figuring out the military piece of Sam's story suggested by the photograph. I did not fully know this at the beginning, of course, but the intriguing portrait of my uncle in his peaked hat turned out to offer a key to the further twists of his life and, through the many layers of mediation that bound him to my father, returned him ultimately to me.

I keep looking, but I cannot find the army registration card for Sam, though I easily located them for my grandfather and his brother on Ancestry.com. After many fruitless searches I learn that, because of Sam's birth date, he was one of a small cohort of men who served in the war but did not register! And so I'm deprived of a possible source from which to seize a crucial missing piece of his biography: precisely where in Russia he was born. I know that I might have discovered this—the name of the town—because the records for my grandfather and great-uncle, who registered around the time that Sam served, give that information: the town, not just the country, Russia.

With one year of high school (as I will discover when I find his service records for World War II—how else would I have learned that?) and one year of military service in World War I, at age twenty-one Sam Kipnis is a young man with no clear idea (my biographer's license) of what to do with himself. After leaving the army with his World War I Victory Medal and World War I Victory Button (all World War I soldiers leave the army with these tokens), he returns home to live with his parents and his little brother at 141 Stanton Street, on the Lower East Side.

Two years later, Sam marries Rose Epstein and becomes the father of a son, Julian, who is born in Brooklyn. By 1930 he has moved to the Bronx with his new family and drives a cab. By all accounts Sam is bright enough, but with little education and no particular training, what is he to do? He works for the Dutchman. Yes, but his little son has severe health problems; he can't breathe in the New York air. Sam doesn't have enough money to move to a better climate, but Julian will die, the doctors say, if they don't get him to the desert.

Three tiny snapshots dated August 1, 1934, less than six months after his father's death, when my mother and father were exchanging love letters, record Sam's venture into his new career, the purchase of the Shamrock Café and Restaurant, at 1539 Sixth Avenue, the only commercial street in South Tucson. The Dutchman, I speculate, before being mowed down in a urinal by a rival mob, gave Sam a stake—money to help the family make a fresh start in the Southwest. I fashion a causal link between these two life sequences: the big gangster on his way out and his one-time little fish collector on his way up. Why not?

The storefront, he writes on the back of the snapshot in Yiddish, "is twenty-five feet wide, and fifty feet deep." He adds, "It has a sixty-person capacity. There's a salon on one side and a restaurant on the other." The storefront windows are decorated with an Irish landscape painted on the horizon. If the name "Shamrock" wasn't explicit enough, the Irish theme is supplemented by a three-leaf clover, which I imagine to be green. The plate-glass windows and the signs attached above the entrance to the café section read like a celebration of repeal: "Happy Days Are Here Again." "Yessir, This is the place." Beer, gin, wines, cordials. The ladies are welcome, too: "Ladies Dining Room" and "Tables for Ladies" are announced in block letters in the window. A narrow strip of sidewalk seems all that separates the commercial enterprise from a littered, unpaved road. Through the window the place resembles the dark, shabby Irish bars that used to punctuate long stretches of Amsterdam Avenue when I was growing up, bars housed in tenements or in the seedy two-story businesses that flourished in Manhattan before gentrification; the kinds of mom-and-pop stores dependent on Mafia protection that my uncle knew inside and out. So, yes, here is Sam, far from New York, and yet oddly at home.

Sam poses in front of the Shamrock Restaurant. "Beer, Wines,

Liquors," it advertises on the window, next to the shamrock logo. "The boss himself," he continues in Yiddish, the self-portrait penciled on the back of the snapshot, "burned by the sun. I feel 100%. More pictures later." On the back of a copy of the same photo—in English, presumably for his American-born brother, my father, who doesn't read Yiddish—Sam varies the riff on the heat: "A hot bartender, 110 degrees. Am I brown?" He is wearing a long white apron wrapped around his waist and is holding his stomach with his hands. "This pose is natural," he writes in the English version. "I had a belly ache." Boss to his mother, bartender to his brother, whatever the language, Sam is thriving in his new life. At thirty-seven, he is only a few years younger than his father had been when he left Russia for America.

In another snapshot, like the self-portrait sent home in a double version, Rose poses outside the Shamrock: "Two waitresses,

talking it over between drinks. Pipe Rose's shoes. She's a good kid." Rose, on the left, and an unidentified woman are wearing white sandals with broad straps and low heels; the white stands out against legs tanned from the sun. Despite the heat, the two women seem happy to stand outside and chat, their hands tucked into the pockets of their crisp uniforms.

I ask the translators about the Yiddish word for "pipe." Sam's verb is *kuk on*: Get a load of those shoes! I'm happy to have the precision but a little disconcerted by what I learn when the translators see the two versions next to each other. In English, to his brother, Sam writes about the waitress: "She's a good kid." In Yiddish, "The shiksa works for us." With the message on the back of the snapshots, I realize for the first time that my uncle writes Yiddish, which binds him to his mother. The tone of complicity reminds me that English wasn't his first language and that, like his parents, Sam was an immigrant, a fact I seem to have trouble holding on to despite the evidence of the photograph from Kishinev. I should also have remembered that the letter from Argentina was addressed to him, in Yiddish. Although Sam ended up in Arizona by accident, because his son could no longer breathe the New York air, its climate suited his gregarious personality: a place to live out one of those uniquely American myths about starting over, where immigrants get to reinvent themselves.

In 1937 the boss of the Shamrock is one of five property owners to petition the county to incorporate the town. He becomes the first elected mayor of the newly, if briefly, independent South Tucson, and he resigns the following year.

In 1939 Sam opens the Ar-Jay Liquor Store. The new storefront advertises "Groceries and Liquors," imported and domestic; a fake street sign attached at an angle to the storefront announces,

"Wines." Rose has a new car. "Look at her!! Does that baby drive now?" Rose poses with the Ford v8, parked in front of the store, purchased from the Ford agency we can see at the end of the street. Is that "baby" the car or the woman? Smiling demurely with one hand lightly resting on the car door, Rose looks pleased with her new purchase. "I can't catch up to her," her husband confesses. That "baby" must be the woman.

"This is the coming street," Sam boasts excitedly in English on the back of a shot of his remodeled storefront, taken in late January, as he dates the snapshot, without including the year. The building façades look freshly bricked. There's a new four-globe streetlight marking a step toward a more urban streetscape. Neon script, Sam points out to the folks at home, announces "Famous Beer" in the shop window, "Imported Groceries." How to convey the importance of his step up in the world? "I hereby introduce evidence #1," he writes at the start of his snapshot dossier, borrowing his brother the lawyer's language to make his case. Look, I'm a success! Here's the proof. "The *boss*," he writes, "the fat guy—now weighs 185 and feels fine." Gone are the captions in Yiddish. Gone is the bartender's long apron: Sam is wearing a spiffy, double-breasted suit; Rose is out of uniform. "During business hours I must wear a coat and tie—but it's hot as hell when you step outside." Four snapshots, with the messages scripted in blue ink on the back, a mini-memoir, convey Sam's hopes for his future, even down to the details of the merchandise on display: "A dated mayonnaise window," he adds proudly, signing off. Is he writing to his mother or his brother? Without the double photographs, I have no way to know.

The War.

The headline reads: "1917 Veteran Now Serves Under Son." In June 1941 Julian enlists in the U.S. Army air corps. He is nineteen, with three years of high school behind him, and single. Less than one year later, in May 1942, his father, identified as the former mayor of South Tucson and the current owner of a thriving business, the Ar-Jay, also enlists. A photograph of the two men appears on the front page of the *Sacramento Bee* on June 4, 1942: "Father and Son Serve." Sam is forty-five, Julian twenty. The photograph and the article have been glued into one side of a dark manila folder saved in my father's drawer.

Father and son, surprised to find themselves thrown together by "coincidence only," belong to the same unit in the army air corps, but as staff sergeant the son outranks the father, a mere private at age forty-five. In the photograph, the grinning father points to his grinning son's insignia: "The boy is top man from reveille to retreat, but after that I can assert myself," Private Kipnis says. Sam explains his reasons for deciding to enlist: "I tried being an air raid warden and doing my part in other civilian defense activities but I finally threw up the sponge and decided to get into this affair all the way." As the California paper recounts the story, army officials state that Sam was accepted into the military at his advanced age because "he served with the 73d Aero Squadron as a sergeant in World War I" and was "overseas in the last war from July 1918 to May 1919." This account is at odds with the information obtained from NARA, which has my uncle discharged from the 1st Co. 152nd Depot Brigade and demobilized at Camp Upton. The insignia on Sam's shoulder in his military portrait does not match that of the 73d Aero Squadron.

Whether or not Sam belonged to this unit, it's a story he told about himself, and told convincingly enough that it made its way into the newspaper. The story's details—the rank, the chronology of years served—had a degree of plausibility considered sufficient by reporters covering the war effort in 1942. When I find myself stuck in contradictory versions, I'm forced to "throw up the sponge," to give up on biographical truth and go in the direction of what's available: "Once you get the air corps into your blood you can't be satisfied until you get back in," the man says. Certainly, Sam longed to be part of the army air force—whether as a repeat of his earlier experience or as a fantasy of joining his son in a flying mission. I've decided to follow him, without knowing.

My grandmother could not have been completely happy to have her son and grandson serving in the war that by 1942 was part of her daily life in the Bronx. Preserved among the ephemera in the drawer is the first page of War Ration Book One, issued in her name: Sadie Kipnis, 2100 Davidson Avenue. The book is dated May 4, 1942, just weeks before Sam enlisted. As identified on the ration card, Sadie is sixty-seven years old, five feet tall, and 138 pounds.

Five stamps remain, hanging like chads in an uneven pattern: twenty-two, twenty, nineteen, sixteen, fifteen.

There is a snapshot of Sadie cradling an infant me the previous year, in Riverside Park, when she was visiting my parents, smiling. But I don't know how to hold these images together, how to create a scenario that would give Sadie a starring role in her own life. But let me at least seat my grandmother at a dark mahogany dining room table as she thinks about the war, pasting the clippings into a folder, closing the folder, putting it in a dresser drawer or a massive sideboard, and hoping for the best.

Her son and grandson served together for sixteen months in a variety of military venues, including training camps, but Julian failed his overseas physical and was discharged in September 1943, just before the birth of his daughter, Sarah. In October 1943 Sam shipped out to the Pacific, where he was made first sergeant. He seemed to thrive in the war and was deployed in the Pacific, on the atoll of Tawara, the scene of a major battle fought primarily by the Marines, but in the less charged aftermath of their triumph.

While still in Sacramento, Sam created and edited a weekly newsletter—"A SQUADRON PAPER IS BORN"—that he dubbed "Beefs and Bouquets." The paper lasted one year during the course of the war, from July 1943 to June 1944, printed even during Sam's brief stint in the Pacific. One day, out of the blue, Sarah sent me a huge envelope with copies of the complete set of the newsletter from the first number to the last, copies that her father had saved and given to her. "Do not know if you will find them interesting or if you get any insight into Sam's mind," she adds in a note, sympathetic to my project to understand the man who was, as always, real to her, a ghost to me.

Sam explained his choice of title in the paper's first editorial, on July 23, 1943: "Where there are no Beefs there usually is no spirit, so let's all get into the spirit and see if we can't change some of the Beefs into real Bouquets." "Beefs and Bouquets" is meant to serve the community—and all are invited to contribute copy. The bulk of the newsletter is made up of crude jokes and cartoons (breasts and "pin down girls" feature prominently), complaints about food, reports on sports teams within the squadron, jokes, birthday wishes. Jocularity reigns.

Beyond the fact of the publication itself—Sam's initiative in creating the weekly newssheet—what stunned me was that the language, tone, style, and matter of "Beefs and Bouquets" so perfectly fit the only way I had ever imagined this aspect of World War II: through the words and music of the musical whose melodies had haunted my childhood, *South Pacific.* I found it hard to realize that someone in my family, my father's brother, had lived and recorded what as a protected child I imagined as entirely remote, or a matter of song and dance, my father singing "Some Enchanted

Evening." It wasn't so much that the newsletter gave me insight into Sam's mind, it was more that I saw my uncle through a scrim of American culture I thought had nothing to do with me. How had my uncle become so completely American, more American than my American-born father? If anything, I was more baffled after poring over the newsletter than I had been before.

The stakes of the war appear in flashes in the mimeographed pages of the newsletter, and occasionally the editor weighs in without a joke. One editorial features a portrait of Sam, pen poised, as he holds forth with a note of authority on serious war talk, echoing the phrases of the era, the subject of "ESPIONAGE": "By talking about moving or going places . . . the professional spy cashes in, and the loose talk that he picks up goes through channels to SPY headquarters. From there on trouble starts brewing. . . . Button that lip. Don't talk."

Sam sent "Beefs and Bouquets" home for almost a full year, but the messages scrawled on them are primarily for Julian, the missing half of the original father-and-son squadron team, whom Sam clearly misses and to whom he addresses the V-Mail. If Sam wrote separately to Rose, those letters are not here. In one of the newsletters, composed in Hawaii, Sam addresses his wife, explaining why, as portrayed in the lead cartoon, one of the hula dancers made a grab for him and pulled him onto the dance floor.

The first V-Mail Sam writes home, dated October 12, 1943, makes clear the persona he has carved out for himself: "Greeting folks from granddad away out in the Pacific. It's warm here and our campsite is situated in a canyon that reminds me of Sabino Canyon. The mountains are pretty but they have nothing on good old Arizona. . . . You no doubt realize that these letters are censored so I will not be able to tell you what the flights are doing. I can tell you that we are set up in fair shape and as usual I'm busy as hell fathering the outfit." The conclusion of this letter, which has several lines blacked out, is a rare reference to the war, beyond the communal life of men: "Lots of love to you all, kiss the baby for me, and be good to Mom. She needs a friend while I am helping clear this world of rats that won't last long since we are here."

Sam sends love to Julian's wife, Ruth, and his own, and kisses to baby Sarah, but the strongest current throughout is the one that ties him to Julian: seeking his approval of the newsletter dated November 10, 1943, worrying about his reassignment, and missing the son he sometimes calls "mate": "It seems only yesterday that you were here with me, yet on your end it must seem like three years," he writes on December 9, 1943. And when he recovers from jungle fever in early 1944 in a hospital in the Hawaiian Islands, he seems to want to console his son: "There is nothing for you to have a heavy heart," he writes about his convalescence. Bizarrely, as if through a reverse act of identification, the father contracts the illness from which his son had suffered in childhood: "Father inherits asthma from son." In his last V-Mail, Sam responds to Julian's query about working together after the war: "So you want to go into business with me? You know I'm crabby and hard to get along with. Are you asking for it?" And then, "Dope out a deal and we will see what can be done."

The last number of "Beefs and Bouquets," dated June 11, 1944, was published in Tucson and refers to itself as the "ex-official poop sheet of the 396th Bomb Sq. Published semi-annually by the now extinct 'ıst Sgt' of the A.C.," and it is signed Sam and Julian Kipnis. This is Sam's farewell to a dozen or so men from his squadron. "To be a civilian," he writes in closing, "is not too easy." Once Sam recovers from his attack of jungle fever, "Pop" and "kid" buy a tourist court in Tucson, a lucrative form of real estate in the area, a purchase duly reported in the *Arizona Daily*

Star. "I'm much better," Sam writes in the final number of the newsletter to one of his war buddies, "and all I do now is sit in front of my office and spin yarns about the war."

Sam's return to Tucson in 1944 made news in the *Arizona Daily Star*. Because of his age, the newspaper reports, "the boys in his outfit called him 'Pop.'" The article repeats the story about World War I service and is generally accurate, except for the erroneous detail of placing the man in the battle famously known as "Bloody Tawara" as a member of the Seventh Air Force. Despite the error of aggrandizement, in 1944 Sam Kipnis is still considered newsworthy.

In the years separating my late-life introduction to my uncle's side of the family from the actual composition of this book—my imaginary encounter with Sam; the real one with his son, Julian, and with Julian's daughter, Sarah—I searched, with a kind of persistent desperation, for the bare facts of this man's biography, details I hoped would somehow bring this missing person out of the shadows. I often felt that I was pursuing a stranger, who at times happened to resemble my father physically to an uncanny degree, so much so that in some of the early photographs, if the two were not posed side by side, I would occasionally hesitate about which of the brothers I was looking at. It wasn't that I doubted the relation. It was more that my mind resisted what I couldn't feel, and what I couldn't connect to a story; there were not, in the beginning, enough links in the chain to forge a reliable narrative, enough invention to fill in the empty spaces of the spline, the metaphor I began with.

If now I glimpse something like a recognizable story line—a familiar immigrant's tale of displacement and renewal—it is because I have already reassembled the bits and pieces of a scattered archive and gathered them into a design of my own.

10. The Lost Scrapbook

My father saved a handful of letters from his brother dated from the time of my grandmother's death in the mid-1950s to the late 1960s. All were addressed to my father's office, even the ones that include my mother in the salutation; all but one close formally, "As ever, Sam" or "Sincerely, Sam." Scrutinizing Sam's letters for what they might reveal about the relationship, I am struck by how little the brothers had in common beyond their genealogy and their name. Still, there is something there, or was, or nothing would have been saved in the first place. This would not be the first tale of brothers, siblings whose paths in adulthood diverged so fully that only a posthumous editing could bring them back together. But it is the one I've inherited.

January 13, 1954, the day after their mother's, my grandmother's, death, the day of the funeral for which Sam does not return, Sam writes to his brother, recalling an anecdote about their father, confronted with *his* father's death: "Did you ever hear what 'Pop' told me after attending grandpa's funeral? I was so impressed," Sam recounts, "that I passed the very same words on to Julian, and if he follows them after I pass on, I will be content." (Neither brother seems to have attended their grandfather's funeral, although at the time they were all living in the same city.) Sam quotes their father's words: "I am taking the rest of the day off to meditate. Tomorrow, I'll carry on as those on earth must do. If in my opinion he was a good father to me, I'll remember him in kindly thoughts. If not, I'll simply say, 'let the old so and so rest in peace.' Can't you just 'see' him as he said that?" I try to see the man Sam evokes behind the twinkly smile my grandfather wore in most of the snapshots of his life in America, and in the humor of his Talmud Torah letters, but only a fragile chain of collected facts and artifacts links these three phantom Kipnis men to me and to each other: Chaim/Harry the somber, bearded ancestor, who peddled stationery on the Lower East Side, known to me only by two photographs and a tombstone; Raphael H., the grandfather bookkeeper who saved his letters in Yiddish and left behind his cigarette case; and finally Samuel R., whose career, such as it was, made it onto the pages of the *Arizona Daily Star*.

My father is strangely missing from this group shot of Kipnis men: my grandfather; my uncle and his little son, Julian; and my great-grandfather, Chaim. Judging from Julian's age, the photograph seems to date from around 1924, the era of the chain-link snapshots. My great-grandfather, absent from that scene, here looks exactly as he did in the 1906 family portrait. An unchanged, man, he is still wearing a hat indoors, and though his grizzled beard has grown whiter, its fan-like shape remains unaffected by time, by the times.

In thinking about their mother, my uncle skips over their father's death, reaching instead for the still older loss, that of their grandfather. But he remembers their father's approach to death: "I am applying the same method again only changing the pronouns to 'she' and 'her.' God rest her soul." Their mother's passing is an occasion for Sam to reflect upon what he owes his brother for the twenty years during which my father had the sole care of their mother, twenty years during which they had not seen each other: "To you I offer my most heartfelt thanks, for 'service above and beyond' your duty, for service on the scene without any reinforcements or financial aid." My uncle offers to carry his share of the burden after the fact, if my father can "reach a monetary tabulation" for his services. Given the straightened circumstances Sam describes the following spring, it is unlikely that the debt was ever repaid in this fashion. And how, anyway, could one ever repay hours of presence, over two decades? The scare quotes suggest that Sam knew that he had moved into a zone beyond accountability. The letter closes with a series of commonplaces about mortality and a note of impersonality: "What is there to say? The aged must go, and the young will go. In the meantime, let's try and stay well and hope for the best." Sam sends best wishes to my father's family.

Despite the clichés and the enigma of this family's estrangements, at my father's funeral, in the place of a eulogy neither of us felt capable of delivering, my sister read aloud Sam's letter to my father. Perhaps we wanted obscurely to substitute one loss for another, to reconnect my father to his family, to close the gap that we had felt but never discussed, though we knew he had a brother, even if we knew nothing about him, least of all what our father might have felt toward him.

One year later, in April 1955, a second letter arrives, two typed single-spaced pages, on letterhead from Elite Enterprises, with a P.O. Box address and a single Saguaro cactus logo. "Dear Louis," Sam begins using my father's full name, signaling the seriousness to come. Sam quickly gets to the point: "Sick and broke. That sounds blunt, but it is the truth." And he paints a bleak picture of his finances and his prospects on his fifty-eighth birthday: "All I've got is the shack I live in, plus a mortgage, and the car Rose is driving, 1952 Chrysler. That's it. I don't know how come I'm writing this, only I'm alone, bills piling up and no outlook." Rose is in New York visiting dying relatives in the hospital, but she is unlikely to phone, Sam explains, "because she will be ashamed," ashamed to tell the truth about Sam. The question Sam fears my father will ask Rose is: "What is Sam doing?"

The pity letter, as I think of it, ends on a desperate note: "Can you help me in some way? Two years ago I heard that you made a big strike at the coast. I was glad for you as you went through quite a mess yourself, and had a family to raise, etc. I would never ask you, but as said before, after I pay the insurance tomorrow, I cannot meet any other bills, and the cupboard is empty. When Rose gets back I suppose she will pawn her ring and sweat it out." I read this plea with a mixture of sadness and bewilderment about Sam's plight—what happened to him after the war, what happened to the first elected mayor of South Tucson?—but also wondered again about the impenetrable layers of family silences.

My father's "big strike on the coast," yes, this was the defining event of my parents' adult life and my adolescence. My father, in a one-time coup, won a lawsuit in California on behalf of minority stockholders against Howard Hughes that brought my father a flash of celebrity and a very large check, which he photocopied and saved, along with a newspaper clipping about the case. So I'm not surprised to see that Sam had heard about the "strike." But what is the mess that I don't remember but that this brother, my uncle, would know about? The door to another mystery opens. I can recapture the spreading sense of promise brought by the scale of the success. The money, longed for by my mother, meant that life would change: deluxe travel to Europe but also something dark, the scent of an affair, around the edges of the new fortune.

The previous fall, my father and his triumphant partners flew back from Los Angeles to New York on TWA's first transcontinental, nonstop flight. Prominently displayed in my parents' apartment was a framed autographed flight map from the trip, above which is mounted a photograph featuring the members of the successful law team beaming at my father. Between the dates of the transcontinental flight and the big check, my grandmother died of heart failure. Did she know of her younger son's accomplishment before she died? One son's success, the other's failure? Did my father send money to his brother? Was he his brother's keeper?

Sam signs this letter, "Anxious."

I sent Sarah the batch of letters that Sam had written to my father, and I received a detailed commentary on Sam's version of history. The plea for money that had troubled me by its pathos left Sarah unmoved: "When Grandpa," as she calls Sam, "gave your father that sob story about being broke and asking for money, it was probably because he wanted to do something foolish. The only reason they had money was because of Grandma [his wife,

Rose]. It makes me angry that he wrote that and saddens me to think that your father might have believed it. The lies he told in this letter are just too much. Nothing like an old fool."

Here's the difference between Sarah and me: For Sarah, Sam was a real person who on many occasions disappointed her. For me, Sam is a character in the story I'm creating, a character for whom I have an almost novelistic attachment. The truth I need about him could come in the form of lies. Whether Sam was really broke or just looking for some extra cash in order to "run around on women" as Sarah always refers to her grandfather's philandering, doesn't matter to me. It matters to my story about the brothers, of course, and makes me wonder whether woman-izing ran in the family. I also wonder whether Sam's hard times drifted down, somehow seeped—unmentioned—into our New York family.

I find it hard not to regard Sarah as my primary authority on Kipnis family matters. She knew Sam as I had not, and she had started a family scrapbook before we met. "I will get my book that I am putting everything in," she replied in response to one of my endless queries about Tucson, "and see what I can come up with." Like Sarah, I'm trying to see what I can come up with, as I put everything into *my* book. Little by little, I'm moving the contents of the drawer into a shareable story.

December 18, 1964, the day before his younger brother's birthday (that goes unnoted), Sam writes to Lou, thanking him for the book my father has sent him: Henry Roth's *Call It Sleep*, which had just been republished in paperback to great acclaim. Sam has not yet finished reading the novel, he says, and turns instead to describe the book about life on the Lower East Side that he plans to send my father after the holidays, *The Spirit of the Ghetto*, by Hutchins Hapgood. The book, he says, is "the best on the old days," all the more "amazing" because it was "written by a non-Jew." The book was given to him by the wife of a colleague—a fellow inspector from the Motor Vehicle Bureau, which is how I learn about another of Sam's many odd postwar jobs. The inspector's wife, "a devout Baptist," collects books to distribute "to the Indians" and rescued this one for their Jewish friend. Sam delineates the table of contents and promises to send my father the book after the holidays.

I looked through the book, trying to figure out what these "old days" on the Lower East Side might have meant to Sam sixty years later, and to my father. "The shrewd-faced boy with the melancholy eyes that one sees everywhere in the streets of New York's Ghetto occupies a peculiar position in our society. If we could penetrate into his soul, we should see a mixture of almost unprecedented hope and excitement on the one hand, and of doubt, confusion, and self-distrust on the other hand."

Did Sam see himself in the portrait of the "little Jewish boy" from the Lower East Side whose education came from the "strange and fascinating life on the street"? Despite Sam's enthusiasm for its accuracy, Hapgood's portrait of the Lower East Side "ghetto" seems fraught with stereotypes, but it's also true that what I missed for the longest time in the 1903 Kishinev photograph was the fearful little boy standing between his parents. Focused as I was on the story of my grandparents as my *father*'s immigrant parents, I failed to notice that the boy, his brother, was an immigrant, too. I never imagined how this boy grew up in America, how he might have felt about his much younger brother being born into English and into education, what becoming an American might have meant to him. Still stranger to me now is that I never thought about how having such a brother shaped my father's identity. There was always something so orphaned, I want to say, about my father's place in our little nuclear family, the family so overshadowed by the Millers, that I never looked to what might have been his attachments.

The rest of Sam's letter describes a life of marginal survival, picking up odd jobs "that buy my tobacco."

The next letter is dated three years later, February 1967. The brothers keep writing, though six letters in thirteen years suggests that the tie requires minimal contact to maintain. It's impossible to know whether my father culled these letters from a wider correspondence, identifying them as worth saving for sentimental value, or whether these were the only letters Sam wrote. If the brothers never saw each other again after 1934 when Sam moved to Arizona, I would guess these are the sole traces of their original relation.

Sam often complains about having no money, and being unemployed and not well. My father, presumably, reports on the many trips to Europe and the island vacations he takes with my mother. "Say, how many months a year do you people spend in New York?" Sam asks. Despite the evident disparity between their lives and fortunes, the thread of connection between the brothers remains on paper, even if nothing came to replace the bonds of life on Stanton Street.

"I believe I have solved a problem," Sam writes in February 1967, "that you mentioned some time ago—the perpetuation of the Kipnis name—you with two daughters and Julian with one daughter. There is just the three of us now, right?" The "three of us," after the deaths of my great-grandfather Chaim and my grandfather Raphael, are the three Kipnis men: my uncle Sam; his son, Julian; and my father.

My father never voiced his concern about the name with my sister or me, even when, as we married, we abandoned the Kipnis tribe without a thought to its perpetuation. We couldn't wait to shed the name that for both of us, by the 1960s, meant a childhood and especially an adolescence of familial constraint. The last thing we cared about in the 1960s was our ethnic roots or carrying on the name that signaled them. We both married non-Jewish men, possibly because we wanted some other kind of marker—something less predictable than "the Kipnis girls" that had labeled and lumped us together for so many years. It's true, then, as Sam feared: the daughters all abandoned the name that the sons had carried on.

When I told my thesis adviser in graduate school that I was changing my name, he asked, always protective of the patriarchal order, "How does your father feel about that?" Acting as my lawyer, my father had taken care of the name-change formalities for me, but it had not occurred to me to ask him the question, and he had not volunteered a comment. Perhaps he had given up on the name when he gave up on his daughters' virginity, by far the harder struggle.

Sam has found a way to save the Kipnis name, to compensate for the generations of daughters. Because he was the "only living survivor of the original five men who petitioned the county to incorporate the town," Sam was invited to make a donation of memorabilia to the archives of the University of Arizona. His collection of clippings, war souvenirs, photographs, and other claims to civic fame have brought Sam Kipnis into History. He doesn't reach for the capital letter, but something like regional American history is on his mind: "the history of Tucson, Pima County and the Southwest." This is no small matter. The Kipnis name "will appear the same as Wyatt Erp in the Tombstone Story—Arizona History." Not bad for an immigrant to find himself "the same as Wyatt Erp," the outlaw lawman hero from this corner of the world. Sam's pride of connection radiates from the page, in the bold, oversize, slightly foreign penmanship that resembles that of his father.

Sam concludes his narrative of accomplishment, which now will enter the public record under his name, the name that joins not only the brothers but father and son, with a touching faith in the redemptive power of the archive: "So I believe with all my faults and mistakes I made in my lifetime Pop would be pleased to hear of my making history here in Arizona—and our name would be remembered for many years to come—I hope you too are pleased." Was his gangster past what Sam was hoping to expiate with his donation?

Do we ever stop hoping that we will please our fathers? What else am I doing here, trying to atone for jettisoning the name, trying to place it in another kind of history?

The same as Wyatt Earp.

Only after excavating Sam's biography through articles and clippings did I begin to realize that there was a shape to his life—to figure it out first on its terms and then in relation to my father. Now, I am astonished to learn that my uncle's story has been deposited in the library of the University of Arizona. "Story," of course, is not quite the right word. But the man had enough of an idea of himself to preserve the recorded traces of his life in the Southwest. Sam seemed to have his collection of memorabilia, his scrapbook, ready to go when he was approached by a field historian from the university in 1967.

In turn, I need to create my own account of Sam Kipnis beyond his role as the surviving representative of a local saga, the "first elected Mayor of South Tucson," a narrative that will place the clippings in a chain soldered by an emotional filler, figure out who else this man might have been. Can I somehow reach down to what lies "under the story," as my yoga teacher likes to say about meditation? Maybe that should be a term: "understory"—not "backstory," with its overtones of Hollywood gossip and glamour. The understory. That would suit these characters in my family, who are something like understudies—practicing for parts that they never quite get to play on stage, or not for long.

I fax the librarians at the Southwest Jewish Archive at the library of the University of Arizona a formal inquiry requesting a copy of the file. I'm especially eager to learn whether my uncle tells any tales about Russia, where exactly he was born, or something more about the early years of my ancestral family, when they were immigrants in New York. While I'm waiting, I check out the archive online. There is an alphabetical list of all those included in their holdings. Accidents of the alphabet: Sam Kipnis is in the same box as Barry Goldwater. Wyatt Earp is indeed nearby. In the interim I learn that despite his place in the Southwest Jewish Archive, Wyatt Earp was not actually Jewish. He was married to Josie Marcus (or lived with for forty-six years), a Jewish woman from San Francisco. Josie, the story goes, loved her gunslinger so much that when he died she had him cremated and buried in a Jewish cemetery. That's how, in part, Sam Kipnis gets to share history with Wyatt Earp.

Finally, the file arrives, suspiciously skinny—like a rejection letter. Inside the FedEx envelope is one page of a double-spaced typed student library report based on the obituary of my uncle that had appeared in the local paper. But where are all the items listed in the letter to my father? I hire a researcher from the university library school to see whether she can track down the file described by Sam and for which Sarah has a letter of acknowledgment. My ingenious researcher, Lynne Collins, finds the receipt of the donation, but the archive seems to have disappeared from the library. My uncle, then, belonged to two archives—the one larger, generic one for Jews of the Southwest; the other that would have belonged solely to him because of his contribution to local history.

"P.S. Are you a Grandpa yet?" Sam asks his brother at the end of his letter.

It's 1967. My sister and I are both married, but neither of us has had a child; neither of us will.

By February of the following year, 1968, Sam's wife, Rose, has died, and Sam replies to my father, who seems to have asked for his news, explaining his current circumstances as a widower, reduced to living in a mobile home in an "adult park." The brochure was enclosed: Fairview Manor—"a new way of life for fun-loving people" in downtown Tucson, "playing shuffleboard and feeling terribly lonesome." His son, Julian, has suggested that he look for "some nice widow" to take to the movies, but Sam has become obsessed with a woman from his past. In going through his wife's papers, he has discovered two letters that this woman had written to him in 1944, while he was still overseas, "begging" him "to let her know" whether he was alive.

"When Rose died," Sarah writes, "Sam went running all over the country trying to find some woman he had a fling with. He didn't know Rose knew about it."

"I just went along working," Sam writes his brother, "and was a boarder in my home for 25 years. Can you understand what I'm trying to tell you?"

Twenty-five years after the war, my uncle reveals not only his obsession with his mystery woman but the nature of his marriage. Bitterly, Sam revisits his grievances: "It was her idea for me to go to war with Julian to get me out of her life so she could have her fun running a very good business and living high on the hog." The business was the Ar-Jay liquor store that Sam had bought in 1939. Sarah disagrees. "When they moved to the bigger store," Sarah said, "Rose started buying new Cadillacs every year. The liquor store made good money. Too bad they sold it, but that was due to the fact that Sam wanted his name in the paper as the first father and son in the service and Rose couldn't keep up with it alone."

Sam's version is the one that made it into the newspaper. "Once you get the air corps in your blood you can't be satisfied until you get back in," Sam is quoted in the *Sacramento Bee*, shortly after enlisting. The paper reads: "Kipnis, who has only the one child, said his wife is agreeable to his reentrance into the military service and that she will run the business until his return."

His wife wanted to get rid of him. Sarah: "It was not Grandma's idea for him to enlist with Dad."

Sam wanted his name in the paper. Sarah: "He wanted the publicity, Grandma begged him not to go."

While Sam was away in the war, Rose, according to Sarah, "moved in with Mary in Snòb Hollow. Mary was a very successful madam in Tucson." (Rose did not live in the brothel, Sarah clarifies, sensing my shock. "Mary had a beautiful home in the foothills.") At some point after the war, Sam and Rose divorced, and then got back together again. Rose, Sam complains to his brother, still angry after all the years gone by, "never wrote a line" while he was in the war. Mystery woman wrote regularly, keeping his spirits up. When Sam returned from overseas, the letters stopped and his marriage resumed. But the breach was not healed.

The truth of the past comes in pieces, but not all of the pieces fit together. The lesson requires relearning.

Sarah wrote, "Grandpa ran around on Grandma with a woman he met in New Mexico. He must not have told her he was married, and she sent letters to the house. He was mad when Grandma died and he found that she had intercepted them." I confess, I like Rose's revenge and believe Sarah's version.

Sam wrote to his brother, "I traveled two months covering Albuquerque, Santa Fe, Colorado Springs, Casper Wyoming, Omaha, trying to find her." Sam ran ads in various newspapers, he tells my father, looking for information about the woman's whereabouts, offering rewards; he tried to trace her following out the names and places he remembered having seen listed in

a little address book of hers that he no longer had in his possession: "Well, all I do is keep thinking whether she is still alive." I
read my uncle's words, wondering what my father made of this
outpouring of need, my father, a man whose open face shut down
into a mask of discomfort at the expression of anything resem-
bling an intimate exchange. Sam: "You and Julian is all I've got
to turn to. Remember, you asked me to write so I'm telling you
my troubles." The confession seems to respond to an invitation,
a standing invitation to my uncle to unburden himself. I will
never know how my father reacted to his brother's pathos, but
he appears to have himself confided his private disappointments
in an earlier letter.

Before signing off, Sam consoles my father about the failure
of my marriage: "Nancy, better to take care of a pimple fast than
to wait till it becomes cancerous, she is still young and she will
be O.K." I am still disturbed to find myself circulating in this
exchange between the brothers, not least in my uncle's metaphors
of wisdom (my suicidal meltdown a pimple). I can't help feeling
resentful, if not surprised, that my father substituted my unhappiness for a more difficult outpouring of his own. But beyond
that annoyance and the belated shame of exposure, there is the
growing sense I cannot repress that this man who fascinates me
by his absence now would not have enchanted me by his presence
then. My love affair is with the quest.

Two years after Sam's sad accounting is the final letter in the
little collection: a printed Christmas card, "and Chanukah" added
by hand, announcing his marriage to another woman, a widow
who, like his first wife, is called Rose. The former neighbors in
the trailer park traded in their individual single-wide trailers for
a double-wide, deluxe mobile home. "Believe me when I tell you,
'it's better the second time around.'" Signed "Brother Sam."

Happy ending for the few years that remained, an unexpected finale that rescued Sam from the abjection of the postwar debacle. Between his pension, social security, and the lovely widow, Sam briefly recaptured something lost, and in a way he started over. In the same letter of despair about the missing mystery woman and the emptiness of his life, Sam brightens with excitement about the donation: "The research on South Tucson is already catalogued and . . . many of the kids are calling for a look see." My uncle has closed the Arizona circle that began with the purchase of the Shamrock Café. What survives is his belief in the scrapbook, the record of accomplishment that in his mind carried the immigrant boy back to his father and forward into American history.

11. Distant Cousins

The scrapbook obsessed me. The receipt proved beyond all doubt that my uncle's donation had been taken into the library's precincts. Why not go to Tucson and see for myself? Maybe by sheer chance I would put my hand on the precious scrapbook that had been there all along, just hidden from sight in a dusty, crowded corner of the library, buried under a pile of forgotten documents. I trusted Lynne, my researcher in Tucson, completely; she was a recent graduate of the School of Information Resources and Library Science and had an insider's knowledge of the library's secret workings. She was also the one who had unearthed the material trace of the gift. But I could not relinquish the scenario of discovering the missing scrapbook myself. I savored the moment in advance—an academic's fantasy, chasing the grail of the killer archival find. I starred in the movie, as I belatedly hunted down the traces of my ancestral roots, the lost history of the Kipnis name.

Besides, I was curious about the city that had been home to my uncle and his family. I had visited Tucson briefly on two occasions before I knew anything about Sam, and I had fallen in love with the desert. An old friend, Bonnie See, who knew my family from the time of my adolescence, had moved there recently. The thought of seeing a friend I had loved in the past (could it have been forty years already?) gave the trip an additional edge and, in a strange way, made the quest more real. My friend knew me when I was still Nancy Kipnis, and she was still Bonnie Rous.

And then there was Brownie. Over the years, in the course of my correspondence with Sarah, she would, faced with a question about the past that she or her mother couldn't answer, say that she'd have to ask Brownie. I managed not to understand for a very long time who Brownie was and, therefore, why she might know what Sarah and Ruth didn't about Sam and Julian. My failure to recognize Brownie's importance as a source of information about my lost family was more than accidental, it was systemic—or rather, more precisely, symptomatic of a chronic distortion in my research. From the beginning I tended to focus exclusively on one side in each family unit: my father's, my grandfather's, my uncle's. No matter how often I was brought up short and forced to realize that the *other* side—my mother's, my aunt's, my grandmother's—necessarily also belonged to the picture, I kept returning, lemming-like, to the male line. Such was the force of my obsession with the Kipnis name and its genealogy. I kept not seeing—deferring, postponing—the women, and yet it was the women who were the guardians of the story I was looking so hard to find. I wasted a lot of time that way, as I doubled back over missed opportunities.

It was not until the long plane ride from New York to Tucson that I finally improvised a tree of relations and figured out not only who Brownie was but also who we all were to each other. Brownie was the niece of Sam's wife, Rose. I knew even less about Rose and her side than I did about Sam, and because I wasn't related to her by blood, I discounted her place in the enigma about the two brothers that I was trying to decipher. As late as the week before my trip to Arizona, I hesitated about meeting Brownie, who lived in a senior residence on the outskirts of Tucson. Not only did she belong to the *other* side, she was ninety-seven. Sarah had told me that Brownie was a sharp, poker-playing woman, who "always had something on her plate." I loved that image of a woman that age with a full schedule. I hoped she would make time for me.

Brownie was the daughter of Rose's sister, Rachel. Rose and Ray, as Rachel was always called, were Epsteins and had emigrated from Poland around the time that the Kipnises had emigrated from Russia. Julian was Brownie's first cousin on her mother's side and my first cousin on my father's. Ergo, Brownie and I were second cousins—by marriage, I added mentally, by marriage, not by blood. Looked at this way, though—having shared a first cousin by blood—I eased my way into embracing a second cousin. Our relation started to feel natural. We shared an uncle. My uncle Sam was also *her* uncle Sam, and hers even more so, since she had actually known him. She had known Julian, too, whom she thought of as her kid brother; he was ten years younger and adored by her mother, Ray. It was confusing to have the family picture expand this way, after a lifetime of our tiny cohort of four Kipnis members on the Upper West Side of Manhattan.

Sometimes, when I tell friends this story, I learn that for many people these distinctions among relationships don't matter. They might say "my cousins" or "distant cousins" and not feel the need to articulate second cousin by marriage, first cousin once removed, even when that was the case. Not me. I'm fascinated by the language delineating degrees of separation. This may have something to do with the oddness of the word "removed," which sounds like an effect of distancing or elimination, whereas in reality, the removal has turned out to be the operative force in my getting closer to the family I had just begun to find. Removal paradoxically made present what had until now seemed entirely absent. Julian's daughter, Sarah, my first cousin once removed, brought me into intimate, even physical touch with what had been eradicated by time and geography: the Kipnis side of the family, including now my second cousin, Brownie. Removed or second, by marriage or blood, these distant cousins have become precious to me, close.

But my earlier punctiliousness about degrees of relation dies hard. I lived for so many years before this genealogical adventure without knowing, thinking, or indeed dreaming of these bonds that I am slow to make them mine. I cling to the strangeness, the estrangement. I have begun to realize, though, that as I take in the stories, it's precisely the stories that make the bonds, and it's time to get over blood.

Almost immediately after touching down in Tucson, I headed with Lynne for the University of Arizona campus, the "U," as everyone there called it, a few blocks from the hotel. After my long hours in air-conditioned planes and airports, I was briefly stunned by the June heat and, as I eyed people walking with sun umbrellas opened over their heads, wished I had remembered to pack a hat; it had been cold and raining (wet umbrellas) in the week before I left Manhattan. Lynne, slender and neatly dressed in black jeans and shirt, strolled along bareheaded, not even breaking a sweat, but then after fifteen years in the city, she had adjusted to the climate. Emboldened by her example, I ignored the burning tips of my ears.

Roger Myers, Associate Librarian and Archivist, with whom Lynne had scheduled an appointment, led us down several floors by elevator to an underground space belonging to the university's Special Collections. I gazed hopefully at the long rows of modern, pale-beige steel cabinets that both he and Lynne had previously consulted. We slowly flipped through the tightly packed and neatly typed file cards, cross-checking under every category we could think of, but the Kipnis name never appeared.

On our way out, like Orpheus leaving the underworld, I tried not to look back at the closed cabinets that housed material marked "unprocessed"—recently arrived documents that awaited attention from the archivists on staff—and for a moment considered begging the librarian to let me look through them. I knew he would say no; I was only postponing the inevitable surrender. Still, Roger kept the photocopies I had brought him of the letters from earlier archivists, now dead, who had officially acknowledged receipt of the donation in 1967. Maybe one day he would find the archive and remember my visit.

The scrapbook, both versions, was gone, and with it not just my uncle's World War II memorabilia but letters from Arizona governors and the head of a Mexican patriotic association and, most intriguing of all, a letter from the legendary New York City mayor Fiorello LaGuardia, born in New York but raised in Prescott, Arizona. All these documents were carefully annotated by hand on the "gift report" that was signed by Field Historian John Gilchriese, thanking my uncle for his "interesting material," just as Sam had written to my father, when he described the donation.

The archive had vanished, Myers said, possibly on its way to being filed. The more likely story about the disappeared scrapbook, and one that I resisted even as I bitterly suspected that I should believe it, was the librarian's speculation that my uncle's documents had actually been thrown away. Despite Sam's belief that the donation had been catalogued, it might in fact never have moved out of archival limbo. Lynne had already mentioned the cynical apocrypha among graduate students, according to which, years earlier, a senior faculty member had amassed something of a private collection of Southwest ephemera, which he sold from his garage. It was hard to know which evaluation was more wounding to my newly fashioned family pride: that the Kipnis archive was valueless and hence destined for the dustbin of history, or that it was valuable as a classic moment of a small town's bid for independence, and therefore appropriated for someone's personal stash of Arizona folklore.

When we stepped out into the brilliant sunshine of the barely fading afternoon light, I momentarily conjured up the happiness on Sam's face, "burned by the sun," as he posed in front of the newly purchased café. "I feel 100%," he had reported home to his brother and mother in 1934. There was, it had started to seem to me, something vivifying about the Arizona sun, its sheer intensity. Despite my sadness about the vanished archive, I felt strangely jubilant in the dry heat, high on the sight of the iconic cacti punctuating the campus landscape. You could almost breathe the desert beyond the sublime Saguaro. No wonder the doctors had sent my cousin here to survive the asthma that had radically circumscribed his childhood freedoms in New York. True, I hadn't found what I had come for, but somehow buoyed by the heat, I felt that the effort to locate the scrapbook was its own reward. I had gone to the end of the quest. There were no more doors to knock on. All the original participants involved with the donation were dead. I could stop now without the lingering anxiety that I hadn't tried hard enough. There would have to be another path to Sam's redemption, his sense that the preservation of the name would make up for his earlier misdeeds and earn his dead father's approval, if not forgiveness. Sarah would be disappointed, since she wanted to pass this piece of the legacy on to her children and grandchildren. Exactly what I was trying to redeem for myself was still not clear to me—my guilt about giving up the name?—though I could feel its driving force.

And, of course, there was also the matter of my hair, a case of minor personal vanity. In Tucson, the lack of humidity magically unfrizzed my tribal hair—the rigid mass that, in my mind at least, always marked me as a Kipnis, signaled my descent from this line through my father's hair, and perhaps also Sam's, before he lost it. In Tucson I could toss my head and my hair would move, ever so slightly, in the breeze.

Just before my departure for Arizona, Lynne had found a link to Brownie's daughter, Sarah Frieden (the two Sarahs had been named after the same great-grandmother on the Epstein side). A few years earlier, this Sarah had published a few lines of family memoir in a special feature in the *Arizona Daily Star* about the Fox Theatre, the town's historic and newly renovated movie house, a reminiscence about her mother's younger days in Tucson: "My father, Joseph Ebner, was the assistant night manager of the Fox Theatre around 1949. My mother, Brownie Ebner, would meet my father outside the Fox at the end of his evening shift so that they could go out for ice cream, or a nice walk." And so when I went to interview Brownie, Sarah naturally also came along. I was at last firmly on the other side, among the women. So what kind of a name is Brownie? I asked Sarah, as we drove to the retirement community where her mother was living. A version of Bryna, she explained, the Yiddish for "blessed," that her mother, Ray, had translated to "Brownie" so that she'd have an American-sounding name. "Brownie" came to predict her size. Never more than four foot eleven, Sarah said; by the time we met she was even smaller, the size of Charlotte Brontë.

"We all had a crush on your father" was the first thing Brownie said to me as we trailed behind her walker-assisted dash from the dining room to her apartment at Broadway Proper. Brownie was five years younger than my father and was recalling a time when she was a teenager living in New York and my father was a young man. This tiny, lively woman piqued my imagination with that brief, unanticipated revelation. Judging by the photographs, the man Brownie knew is the father I prefer, a boyish, still adolescent figure in his early twenties, probably just before he met my mother. But in my rush of pleasure and surprise, I lost this moment to ask her more—about him and his attractiveness, about whether she knew his mother or my mother. I had come to ask about Sam and Tucson, not about New York. I was afraid to pull on that tantalizing thread, the New York story, and watch the sleeve of the interview I had come for unravel.

"So what do you know?" Brownie began, immediately taking charge with an authority that charmed. "What do you want to ask me?" Lynne, Brownie, Sarah, and I installed ourselves around the small dining table, with my portable tape recorder in the middle, next to a large tape recorder with which Brownie listened to audiobooks. Macular degeneration combined with glaucoma had affected my cousin's close vision but not her memory or her mind. The impeccably neat apartment was decorated with framed family photographs and a significant array of tchotchkes—vases with dried flowers, small dishes—in multiples, reminiscent of my mother's decorating style. Her daughter's artwork hung on the walls, and a group of small stuffed animals and pillows lined the edge of the couch.

I told Brownie the little I knew, based on the pages of the *Arizona Daily Star*, and the research I had done along with Lynne. From Brownie I wanted something else, a window into what was neither there, nor, I suspected, in the collection of clippings about Sam's history-making election as mayor. I wanted to know what

Sam was like as a person in the early years of South Tucson, what had happened to him after the war, and why he and my father, despite the letters my father had saved, never saw each other again, once Sam remade his life in the Southwest.

"Uncle Sam was not a great wage earner," Brownie began in her unsentimental way. "He drove a cab, he was a great talker, but he didn't do much in the way of making money." So how could Sam, our perennially underemployed uncle, afford to buy a bar? That wasn't complicated, Brownie explained. It was all about Sam's "connections back east." She continued, "They came out with a couple of thousand dollars—a lot of money in those days." I had guessed nervously that Sam had bought the bar with Mafia money. He might even have had part-ownership in the business, the liquor store, Brownie added, without skipping a beat. Brownie, like Sarah, my Memphis cousin, acted as if Sam's gangster involvement was an utterly normal circumstance.

As she revisited the 1930s, Brownie was specific about money and what people did to earn it—how much Sam paid her mother, Ray, to care for Julian, how people lived "in those days": sharing with other family members, or as boarders to make the rent, often moving to find cheaper or, occasionally, nicer apartments. Growing up in New York, Brownie had attended twenty different schools before reaching high school, she said. She had lived all over the city—"Coney Island, Brighton Beach, you name it." All Brownie's details, material and psychological, had that quality of absolute, unsparing clarity—"I'm not pulling any punches." This included remarking with honesty about what she didn't know ("I couldn't say"), or about what prompted skepticism ("I doubt that") as I sketched out an overly ingenious theory. She knew what she remembered and what she didn't.

I asked Brownie about how Sam came to work for the crime family. Her mother, Ray, as I had heard from Sarah in much the same language, worked in a barbershop where she "manicured Mafia men." One day she offered them the services of her brother-in-law Sam: he could drive a car and had time on his hands. They came up with "enough salary to make it interesting for him." In Brownie's account, which in all points echoed Sarah's, working for gangsters was a fact of life. You had to earn a living. However smart (on Sam's being smart, the two women agreed), my uncle was an immigrant with a minimal education and the father of a seriously sick child. It was the Depression. How many times, growing up, had I heard that phrase, said exactly that way by my parents, never fully understanding its explanatory power for the course lives took in the 1930s.

Little by little I have come to accept this story about my uncle, the minor crime family member, but at the same time, I can't seem to fully believe that I believe it. Hasn't this been the problem all along: how do you come to reimagine yourself in a history you did not know you belonged to? I am closer than I had ever dreamed to this unmet uncle, who read and wrote Yiddish, who flourished in a town whose population was probably smaller than that of a Manhattan apartment block, and who, as a young father, hung out with shady characters at the fabled Cotton Club. And yet.

In so many ways, Sam's story is a quintessential assimilation story of outsider to insider, backlit with the same kind of obscure gangster messiness that was folded into the foreign names in the ancestry of Fitzgerald's troubled American, Gatz to Gatsby. I find myself turning back somehow to re-create myself, the nice, Jewish middle-class girl that I was, as related to that history through this man who once was a crucial part of my father's life. Sam's story forces me to acknowledge the seams that were hidden from view but always just on the other side of the bourgeois family fabric that clothed us: the slightly tatty immigrant lining.

Sam's café, The Shamrock, quickly became the gathering place for the handful of men (including Spanish Americans, as they are described in the local paper) with political ambitions, men who as property owners saw a financial advantage in the town's incorporation: lower taxes, fewer laws regulating the sale of liquor, and the establishment of tourist courts. After the primaries, reports the *Arizona Daily Star* in 1937, my uncle found himself "surrounded by friends in an impromptu celebration at his café across from the town hall"—clearly, a convenient location.

"Sam and Rose prospered," Brownie said about the Shamrock years. "They were kind of smart. They got on to things." Sam had learned about the liquor business from his years with Dutch Schultz, and he had the personality to go with the job. "He loved to lean on his elbows and kibbitz, spout ideas. He had a lot of original ideas." The proprietor of a nearby tourist court was skeptical, Brownie said, about the new owner of the Shamrock. "That Jew won't last there very long," Brownie recalled him saying. "That Jew won't last there very long; that Jew won't make it." I was startled by the word "Jew," but before I could express my surprise, she added with the faintest edge of shared triumph in her voice, "But that Jew did. He made it." The words hung in the air with a sense of absolute truth. I felt in that moment that I was touching, almost tasting the past, with the flux of emotions that had to have been alive in the volatile mix of people, money, and political ambition in South Tucson.

So what about that Jew? There was something about the way Brownie, petite and fragile but intellectually robust, leaned on the word, repeating it, that made me see Sam through his

past—almost back through to the Yiddish-speaking child he had
to have been in Russia, the uneducated immigrant in New York,
and the Jew in South Tucson. I loved her portrait of our uncle as
a man who could "sell you the Brooklyn Bridge." She said, "He
was very convincing," and I was moved by her palpable pride in
Sam, by her admiration for his achievement.

In none of the articles about the South Tucson saga were
any of the personalities described in ethnic terms, except for the
Spanish Americans. One of the most successful businessmen in
the town, I discovered by accident at the Arizona Historical Society,
was Chinese, and in addition to Chinese markets and restaurants,
he had founded a civic association for fellow immigrants. In my
telephone interview with Dave Devine, whose articles I had read
about the period, the journalist said he did not find it surprising
that my uncle's immigrant status wasn't mentioned. "They were
all immigrants," he said. The area had been settled by Europeans
hoping to make their fortune. Sam would not have "played up
the matter of his origins," the reporter reflected. "He would have
wanted to blend in." On the other hand, Devine said, Jews had
been prominent in Tucson for a long time, from the nineteenth
century, and key to the city's economic development. One of the
"merchant prince" families founded the most important local
department store, Steinfeld's, in 1906. But at the same time,
Jews were discriminated against and excluded, until the 1940s,
from the country club, a familiar paradox along the road of Jewish
American assimilation.

It's hard to know how much Sam's immigrant and Jewish
background mattered in the prewar years. The story in the *Arizona Daily Star* recounting Sam's relinquishing of the "marshal's
baton" when he resigned appeared juxtaposed to the headline
"Dodd Attacks Hitler," and later, in 1938, the newspaper ran a

front-page story with the headline "Sudeten Tucson Writhes in Contemplated Coups D'Etat." Ambassador William E. Dodd had resigned his position in late 1937 because of his outspoken criticisms of Hitlerism, and he continued to speak out against the anti-Jewish policies of the Third Reich. Was anyone making the connection with the reports of annexation and anti-Semitism in Europe and the Jewish identity of the former mayor, "that Jew," in South Tucson? The juxtaposition is provocative.

After his brief tenure as mayor, my uncle shared his regrets in public. Coached or improvised, in his letter of resignation Sam covered his disappointment in not succeeding in the battle for the town's autonomy by plucking the fitting cliché from the classic all-American repertoire: "I always will cherish the many hours that we sat in council and directed the affairs of the best and biggest little town anywhere." The *Arizona Daily Star*, a fan neither of the little town's desire for incorporation nor of my uncle's leadership in that drive, sketched a not entirely flattering character profile: "Never one to hide either his own or the town's light under a bushel, Kipnis' outspoken stand on practically every controversial subject that arose earned him the enmity of a number of his fellow citizens." But despite the aspects of Sam's manner that irritated many, his resignation, the *Arizona Daily Star* had to concede, caused "real regret" among his fellow council members, who realized, perhaps belatedly, that "whether his actions had been right or wrong, they had been sincere." The town's character was of a piece with the man's personality: a man of big ideas within a small, scrappy corner of the Southwest, a place where, as Devine described it politely, people came "to let off steam."

The mayor's resignation "was the climax of a day given over by South Tucsonans to meetings," the *Arizona Daily Star* reported.

"These took place up and down the streets, in this office and that tourist court, out on the sidewalks and under the canopies of filling stations." It was easy to visualize the intense human traffic politicking within this postage-stamp municipality, whose urban geography reflected the heart of the exploding car culture in the Tucson area. A traveler to California would stop at one of the many tourist courts on Route 66, spend the night, fill up the tank, have tires repaired, get drunk, and move on the next morning.

When Sam and Rose sold the Shamrock and bought a liquor store in 1939, they called it the Ar-Jay—using Rose and Julian's initials. "They wanted to get away from the bar," Brownie said, "but they wanted to sell bottled liquor." To sell liquor in Tucson, you also had to sell food. So they cooked. "Sam was good in the kitchen," Brownie said, and "they cooked Jewish dishes." Tucson had become a popular place for making movies about the Wild West (filming for the movie *Arizona* began in 1939), and as Brownie recalled, "actors and actresses liked to come in," attracted by the food and the atmosphere of a New York delicatessen. The Ar-Jay was diagonally across the street from one of the fancier Tucson hotels, the Santa Rita, and was in Tucson proper, in an attractive downtown neighborhood, on East Broadway. The move up to Tucson from South Tucson meant a great deal more than a matter of city blocks. It was another world, a world away from the scruffy microcosm of tourist courts and filling stations.

"You won't find what you are looking for," Brownie said, trying to forestall disappointment on my part, when we first spoke on the phone. "There's nothing there anymore."

Seventy years later, Lynne and I scrutinize the storefront of an abandoned business that she thinks might have been the site of the old Ar-Jay. Streets have been renumbered, and so it is difficult to be absolutely sure that we are standing in front of the same place. But many of the architectural details that Sam identified on the back of his snapshot remained, albeit altered by the passage of time, especially the cut-out portions of the roof design sharply visible against the bright Tucson sky. The gleaming black tiles had long since disappeared, but I could picture the mayonnaise jars pyramided in the display window, a snapshot of which Sam sent home as proof of his success.

The longer I stare at the empty storefront—according to the signs in the window, one failed business has replaced another failed business—the more I feel the hopelessness of the task at hand. Maybe Brownie was right. What has my coming here brought me? And so I find myself returning to the snapshots. Perhaps more than the thing itself, those miniature black-and-white images, poignant snippets of Sam and Rose's ambition, carry the truth of that story.

What happened to Sam after the success of the Ar-Jay? Why did he give up what Sarah described as a "gold mine," a business the couple finally sold to a man who became, as she phrased it, "very, very wealthy"? Why did he decide he had to go to war?

Brownie was reticent here. "Sam wanted to be a first in every-thing," she began, taking a stab at the question. He wanted his name in the paper, Sarah had said. He was enamored of his idea of being the only father-and-son team from Arizona to serve in the war. At first Brownie objected that Sam hadn't served—and pointed to an image of her husband, who had been severely injured overseas and who never fully recovered. Clearly, Sam's service had not counted in her memory as particularly significant; she was surprised that he had actually been to the Pacific. And after?

"I wasn't here in those years," she said. These were the years of Sam's decline, after the war, when she had moved back East for a while. "He lacked follow-through," was all she was willing to say, a little sadly.

What remained vivid about Sam for Brownie were the early years, the Shamrock followed by the Ar-Jay, enterprises in which her mother was involved. "Everyone worked in the business," she said of Sam and Rose's knack for exploiting family relations. "Not me though," setting herself apart. Whatever the man's flaws, she had saved him in memory as someone precious to her. I didn't have a father, she said simply, mentioning in passing that her father had abandoned her mother when she was a very little girl, and Sam occupied that role for her. The "most intelligent of her uncles," he listened to her, gave her advice; he was there for her.

With the precision that characterized her comments throughout, Brownie insisted that the version of the past she was offering me was her own: "Everyone sees it from a different angle," she said. "I saw from the outside." Brownie's vision and hearing were both impaired, but the assurance of her narrative voice, I want to say, her fluency as a storyteller, erased any doubts I might have had about her memory. Her Sam, funny, warm, available, was quite dramatically the opposite of the man Sarah saw as distant and cold. How could it be the same person? Naturally postmodern ("We all see the story from a different side") and naturally skeptical ("How can you account for how people behave?"), Brownie created a portrait of Sam and signed it.

I wondered which of the two Sams I would have known. Perhaps Sarah, who was convinced that both her father and grandfather wanted her to have been born a boy who would carry on the Kipnis name, suffered from Sam's postwar disappointments. Perhaps in his role as uncle, Sam simply enjoyed the company of his lively, independent niece, who had witnessed his early successes in Arizona and admired him for them. However radical the difference in their personal relations with him, the women agreed on two things about Sam: he had lots of ideas and he was "a darned good cook." Sarah could still remember the taste of his chocolate pies and twisted cookies that "melted in your mouth."

I could not get Brownie to reflect on the questions that plagued me, especially the one that made this chapter of the family history so dramatic, even melodramatic, to me: *why did the two brothers never see each other again?* My grandmother never saw her parents again, or her sister in Argentina. There was in this family, and in so many others like it, an entire map of severance and separation.

When Brownie described Sam's decision to move to Arizona in the 1930s, she said, jokingly, that it was still the Wild West: "For New Yorkers, Indians were running around with bows and arrows." In the 1940s, enamored of playing cowboys and Indians in Central Park and proud of my brown suede cowgirl outfit, a skirt and a vest with fringes, I would have been excited by the idea of a family out West.

Despite Brownie's reluctance to speculate, I kept coming back to the separation, the brothers. My pet theory: had there been a rupture between the two men, the gangster versus the lawyer? Brownie shrugged, "They were so different, in age, in location, in everything." True enough. It didn't seem an interesting question to her. "I don't remember ever seeing Lou here," she added about my father's lack of presence in Tucson, "or hearing Sam say much about him. He never said, my brother this, my brother that." And maybe she was right. Maybe there was no more to the mystery than those simple facts. They were different. But then Brownie was seeing Sam from the side of the Epstein clan. To her, surrounded by aunts, uncles, and cousins on her mother's side, the story of the two Kipnis brothers was far from paramount. As she said, we all see the story from a different side: from mine, what continued to loom was my father's silence about his brother, who clearly was a lively character—the complete absence of Sam, even as a story, from the family I had grown up in. It was as though my father had edited out, pruned, an entire branch from the tree.

In *The Last Gift of Time*, Carolyn Heilbrun describes the late-life surprise of meeting cousins on her father's side, encounters generated by the publication in the *New York Times* of an article about her retirement as a professor from Columbia University. Unexpectedly she discovered the existence of her father's lost relatives, a family, as she puts it, "in no sense lost, except to me"; and she notes with regret at this belated discovery that "there were generations of women in my father's family I had never heard of, never known."

As Brownie told me stories about her mother, her cousins, and indeed her own long life, I had an aching sense of double belatedness. On the one hand, here I was pursuing my father's side of my family, of which, like my friend Carolyn, I knew nothing. And I found myself asking, as she did then: "Which was stranger: that I never knew my father's family, or that I never wondered why I did not know them? My mother's family sufficed—it was large; it surrounded, sometimes engulfed my childhood; and my father seemed, if I thought about it at all, a part of that maternal clan." On the other, until now I did not make a connection between Carolyn's revitalized family genealogy and my own. I do not seem to have wondered whether I, too, had lost cousins on my father's side whom it would have been interesting to know, even when I met one of her new cousins (actually, a cousin's wife). More than twenty years after my father's death, like my friend I am coming to know the women of that other side, but it's too late to tell her.

I came upon this reflection of Carolyn's by accident, recently, while looking for something I remembered her having said about how dangerous it can be, in one's sixties, to engage in a kind of writing to which one isn't accustomed—in her case, a biography of Gloria Steinem. Working on this book—a departure from my usual practice as a literary critic—I've occasionally feared that perhaps this was the wrong time in my life to take the risk of composing a family biography with so little evidence to go on. But how much more I would have risked losing by not taking that chance, and then, of course, there is no more time for it to be right.

I also asked Brownie about Julian, her cousin and mine. Why he had changed jobs so often, why he had treated his first wife so badly, why despite a chance at education with the G.I. Bill immediately after the war he had waited almost ten years to attend college. And then, as my research into his strange, undated résumé revealed, why had he never finished his degree—a fact he failed to share with his wife and daughter? By her own account, Julian had been a charming child, funny and smart—"he had a lot of Sam in him"—but as an adult, he turned out to be a rather "self-centered person, a lot of ego." The thread of restlessness connected father and son. "Grandpa was a smart man," Sarah had often said about Sam in our conversations; unfortunately, "he never stayed with one thing." Her father, she added, "followed in his footsteps." The two Kipnis men shared a temperament: "they jumped from one venture to another. So many jobs and businesses," and, Sarah sighed, with a note of sad irony, "they got out of the ones that proved to be very profitable." Nothing fails like success, a witty literary critic once said. Maybe that was Sam's problem. And after his, Julian's. Success has a way of wearing off. You conquer one thing and then what? On to the next. As Julian wrote on his résumé, by way of explanation for his new job search: "Insufficient challenge."

When I pressed Brownie to say why she thought Julian had turned out the way he did, she invoked the story of his childhood. For reasons Brownie could not fully explain, Sam and Rose persuaded her mother, Ray, to care for Julian in Tucson for several months, as the couple prepared to leave New York. Julian's subsequent development from delightful child into the somewhat feckless character he seems to have become might have "stemmed from that." Perhaps, Brownie said, he continued to be affected in later life by that sense of abandonment in childhood. Despite the fact that Ray was a "loving aunt" and had "adored Julian," Julian must have felt his mother's absence. Even later, when Sam and Rose moved to South Tucson, given how busy both were launching the businesses—the Shamrock, the Ar-Jay—"how much parenting did they do?" Brownie wondered.

Everything about this part of the Julian story remains on some level inexplicable or at least opaque. Why couldn't Sam and Rose leave New York and take care of Julian themselves? Why did Ray accept to leave her own daughter in New York and instead care for her nephew in Arizona at her own expense? No one seems to know, but it happened, and its aftereffects never dissipated in the minds of those whose lives Julian touched.

Perhaps the ultimate psychic expression of Julian's childhood trauma, if that's what it was, turned out to be the novel he had told me about when I visited him. I had doubted the book's existence. But after Julian's second wife died, her daughter collected his papers, which included the manuscript of the novel, and delivered them to Sarah. "Well, here is your fiction story for today," Sarah wrote when she forwarded my copy. Closing the circle of storytelling that she had drawn for me, Sarah concluded that her father's "imagination got the best of him."

Looking back at the notes I had taken in Memphis, I quickly realized that the stories Julian had told me about his killing seven men (one with his bare hands), stories about his postwar career that I struggled to believe, were the stuff of the novel he had in fact written. *Is Your Daddy Home?* (code for agents making contact) was, as he had said, the title of his one-hundred-page thriller. In it, Julian's alter ego dispassionately drowns one of his victims in a bathtub and eliminates six others with a special weapon that kills silently with a poison needle, on touch, leaving no traces. His wife annotated the narrative with comments suggesting that she believed in its veracity: "I would name this 'Unfinished Diary of An oss Man,'" she wrote on the title page, "if I had that privilege."

I wish the novel had been in my possession while I was in Tucson with Brownie. I'm sure she would have enjoyed hearing about our cousin's literary efforts. Julian was not a great stylist, I would have told her, but occasionally he rose to the level of the genre; he even quoted Hemingway correctly about "the hunting of men." Brownie would have smiled at the ambition of the quotation.

As she reflected on Julian's uprooting, Brownie analogized to her own feeling of having been neglected when she was a small child in New York, forced to move from one apartment to another and often left in the care of relatives or strangers. "Two waifs" was the phrase she used when she linked her childhood feelings to those of Julian, whom she thought of when young as her "kid brother."

Ninety years later, recalling herself through Julian, Brownie still dwelled on the fact that her mother had left her with strangers throughout her New York childhood. "I resent my mother a lot," she said calmly but fiercely, as she resurrected the loneliness of a child whose parents could not or would not look after her.

That injury had not been healed by time. From the force of that memory, Brownie sketched out her life after graduation from high school in 1929. "I wanted to be a teacher," Brownie said, but neither she nor her mother knew about scholarships to college, and so, like one of her aunts who guided her, she trained to operate a comptometer (a complex mechanical calculator) and took the path of business and work.

If I heard then a regret about the narrative of her life, as our time together began to wind down I pushed on past her story to my question, the conundrum of the two brothers who never saw each other again—this, after all, was the heart of the matter, what I had come for. But then, almost as if reframing, rerouting the shape of our exchange and reversing the flow of questions, Brownie abruptly asked: "Was your father a good father?"

Was my father a good father? I froze. I had come to find out what *she* might have thought about my father, not what I did. Was my father a good father? I waffled about my parents' marriage, my father's capitulation to my mother's regime. I realized sharply, as I had at various points in the conversation, that all along Brownie was not only telling me something else, telling me her own story, a story of her family and her place in it, she was also leading me back to mine.

"Am I a loving mother?" she asked with a smile, turning to her daughter, in the wake of my babble. Sarah laughed sweetly in reply and, wisely eluding the question that I hadn't finally answered, said that she wasn't "going there." I remembered my mother mocking her mother, "if I'm not a good mother, who is a good mother," hoping I would acknowledge that she, my mother, was a good mother. Perhaps these are not questions to be asked or answered, perhaps because one can never answer for the other.

As the conversation wound down along with the tape, Brownie elegantly returned us to the business at hand. "This book you're writing, it's going to be . . . ?" She left the query hanging and then, before I could answer, added with a hint of quiet pride, "I liked to write, too."

part 3

Memoirs of a Wondering Jew

12. My Kishinev Pogrom

Turov had been like Kishinev after the massacre, like Bessarabia, like Nanking, like Constantinople, humans destroying one another like hurricanes through houses: babies torn to pieces or fed to dogs, streets piled with corpses and people on their way to being corpses, toddlers clinging to the hands of their dead mothers, and police officers looking away, poking a stick through promising debris. | Amy Bloom, *Away*

Before I traveled to Eastern Europe, I would have been unable to locate the city of Kishinev on a modern map. Kishinev was a place name that came belatedly, when I was already a middle-aged adult, as an overlay to my childhood vision of the Russian Empire. It wasn't yet Chisinau, the capital of Moldova, consistently referred to in the newspapers as the poorest country in Europe, known for sex-trafficking, the illegal sale of bodily organs, and Twitter-assisted post-Soviet turmoil. By the time I decided to visit the long-ago kingdom in 2008, many hundreds of assimilated, third-generation descendants of the vast emigration from Russia at the turn of the twentieth century had, like me, begun looking for their ancestral towns, and Web-based organizations like Jewishgen.org had designed Internet engines to facilitate the research and the journey.

My guide Natasha mapped an itinerary for my "roots-seeking

trip," as she liked to call my quest, that would bring me first to Chisinau (in Moldova) and then to Bratslav (in Ukraine). I would see the places my ancestors had lived in and left. I had already created a minimal script from the scraps of immigration history I had uncovered in the United States. But I wanted more, something that would make the lost lives feel real, at once from there and somehow mine. I did not know exactly what that might be, though I hoped for evidence from the local archives. For that, Natasha explained, I would have to engage a genealogist, and she recommended her colleague Alla.

Even before I left New York for Kishinev, Alla had identified traces of my family lines, archival records of paternal Kipnis relatives, and sent me photographed documents, along with her translations, via e-mail. In the "metrical books of Jewish marriages" Alla had located the marriage in 1885 between Avrum Ber Kipnis (age twenty-four) and Shrifa Greenstein (age eighteen), "daughter of Kishinev *meshchanin.*" Avrum was my great-grandfather Chaim's first cousin, Abraham. The man, his wife, and his children (whose births are noted in the "alphabetical book of the Kishinev rabbinate") sailed for New York from Odessa, a few weeks after my grandparents left Kishinev, on the same ship, the Potsdam, departing from Rotterdam. On the manifest, the cousin's destination is written as 96 "Elin" Street, the home of my grandfather Raphael Kipnis, at 96 Allen Street.

Despite an initial disappointment that the archivist hadn't led me more directly to what I wanted to know about my grandparents—where they married, where their first son was born—she had nonetheless brought me something important: a family connection to the world of Kishinev Jews.

You only think you know what you are looking for. The corollary to that early lesson of the roots quest is this: *what most often proves valuable is almost never what you were expecting.*

Over and over, as I tried to pierce the mystery of this vanished universe, I made discoveries that I could appreciate only once I relinquished my conviction that I already knew what I needed to find. For instance, in her first report from the archives, Alla also described a child. *"1. f.211, inv.11, d.383, p. 263 inv.-264. It is a metrical book with the deaths for 1901. #680 (number of registration). The child without any name of the bourgeois from Tulchin Refuel Kipnis died of convulsions on October, 18, 1901. He was alive for only three days."* Could this Refuel be my grandfather Rafael? Tulchin was a town a few miles from Bratslav, where my grandfather was born. But Rafael "from" Tulchin doesn't have to mean born there, Alla explained; "from" could mean either residence or origin. This infant without a name *might* be the unnamed child listed on my father's birth certificate, where my grandmother is recorded as having given birth to three living children.

What might it have meant for my uncle and my father to know that they had a dead brother between them, and for me—another uncle I would not have known?

Natasha isn't there, nor anyone from the plane, when I enter the small waiting room at the Chisinau airport. (Where have all the others gone so fast? Why am I the only one here?) As I hunt frantically for her cell phone number, a tallish, blonde, slightly plump woman sweeps me up and out of the small airport and into a car, an ancient BMW belonging to friends she has just run into. Natasha radiates a kind of bustling self-confidence, and I feel no hesitation in turning myself over to her, completely.

With me in the front of the car next to Victor, and Natasha piled in the back with her girlfriend, and all the suitcases, we pass through the "gates" of Chisinau, two gigantic apartment towers, with notched profiles flanking a four-lane highway that leads into the city. The high-rises are the signature architecture of the long Soviet presence and the reconstructions of the postwar. As we drive through the modern city on the way to the hotel, I realize with a small shock of distress how little I have thought about this place in its present tense, Chisinau today.

Natasha's friends drop us off at The Dacia, a mid-range hotel in a pretty tree-lined neighborhood near parks and embassies, but that first night we stay just long enough to leave my bags in the room because Natasha has invited me to join her at a rooftop barbeque party. This building, where friends of hers have bought an apartment, is distinctly more luxurious than the projects that line the main road into the city. The apartment belongs to Victoria and Serge, a couple who run a financial newspaper. It's Victory Day, commemorating the defeat of fascism, as they put it. The guests have been toasting each other and, with a strong dose of self-irony, singing songs from their Soviet youth. The war in this post-Soviet world is still an important, living marker, a personal reference of loss—a father, grandfather, uncle. The friends are in a fine mood, though, and acting in a way I have always fantasized about as Russian (indeed, they are all speaking Russian, not the newly official "state language," that's actually Romanian): exuber- ant, emotive, expansive. The friends, mainly academics, belong to the nation's intelligentsia, but "everyone," Natasha says (except, I guess, the hosts), works two or three jobs to make ends meet: salaries are very low, no matter what the degrees.

After a while Natasha and I follow Victoria downstairs to look at the apartment, done up elegantly by Victoria herself in a kind of modified Art Nouveau style—lots of sculpted wood, doorframes, armoires. Victoria brings out her family photo album. Her ances- tors are Russian, and most of the family members are aristocrats. I'm moved by Victoria's determination to keep the family narrative alive. Studying the unfamiliar faces in her album, I wonder what makes it possible to share a family history, and I feel a rush of embarrassment about my matching desire.

"*Amerikanka* looking for her babushka," is how I hear Natasha introducing me when I show anyone who expresses the slightest interest (I show Victoria, of course) a photocopy of the portrait of my grandparents taken in Kishinev that I brandish by way of justification. This is the origin of my search. Natasha reports that the elderly citizens who remain in the local community of Jews whom she interviewed on my behalf before my arrival recognize my grandmother's family name, Scholnick, but not the name I'm researching and that I grew up with, Kipnis. Fixated as I had been from the beginning on my father and his name, I did not attempt to reconstruct the Scholnick line, for which I had even fewer points of departure—or so it seemed at the time. My blindness in this matter is beyond repair, except for the acts of reinterpretation that I undertake now—*Amerikanka* looking for her babushka. Perhaps like my uncle Sam trying to redeem himself in his dead father's eyes by depositing his scrapbook in the library, I do the same in these pages, retrieving the lost names.

I meet the genealogist—young, tall, blonde, a student of architecture. Alla was trained in the National Archive of Moldova but now freelances for foreigners like me. Sitting in the lobby of the Hotel Dacia, perched next to me on the stiff, faux-leather banquettes under the dim light thrown by the giant chandeliers hanging from the double-height ceilings, Alla explains more fully the word *meshchanin* that has piqued my curiosity. Petit-bourgeois, the lower rungs of the ladder of the bourgeoisie, small shopkeepers, artisans, tradespeople. Nothing grand but not laborers or factory workers either. Alla has also found evidence of these Kipnis cousins' children—birth records for two girls. She hands me the documents and rushes off to study for her exams.

"Jewish Kishinev with Jewish Memorial and Jewish Cemetery," the excursion is coded on the itinerary. We are going to follow the path of the pogrom. I've read about the pogrom in Bialik's famous poem "City of the Killings," of course, and in historical accounts describing the events that took place in Kishinev over two days, Sunday, April 6, and Monday, April 7—Easter 1903. The pogrom has been so thoroughly dissected that I feel as if I've lived through it in my imagination. Still, it's the place itself I'm after—the way the streets meet each other, the circuit of the violence, and the architecture of the houses themselves, where people cowered in courtyards or climbed into attics and cellars, trying to hide from the attackers.

The pogrom topography is about a mile long, concentrated in a space that on a map looks a bit like a narrow island, bordered by the River Byck, the poorest area, that in 1941 was the heart of the Jewish ghetto. The streets are dusty and unpaved, and most of the houses have not been renovated. It is tempting to picture life in this area a century ago—crowded streets, large families, before and even during the pogrom. There would not be anything particularly distinctive about this part of town, if there hadn't been the pogrom, the reporting, and the commemoration. We stop in front of a one-story building, with a sloped attic roof and a crumbling façade, the house in pogrom history that in 1904 gave V. G. Korolenko, a Russian writer, the title of his article "House No. 13: An Episode in the Massacre of Kishinieff," a detailed and graphic description of the physical violence. Natasha takes a picture of me in front of it. I'm a tourist, after all, in search of the pogrom I've read so much about. The house number plaque looks newish, but the building feels abandoned; weeds sprout from beneath the sloping cement front steps.

In 2002, the year before the pogrom's centenary com-

memoration, an Israeli academic gained entrance to the courtyard of the famous house, but since then the courtyard has been
locked to outsiders. There's a little grocery store next door, with
new windows, and at the end of the street, signs of imminent
gentrification. According to one of the accounts of the pogrom,
eight Jewish families lived around the courtyard behind the house,
and the compound included a grocery store. I take a picture of
the closed door, and of the store. Bialik's poem urges its readers
to travel there, to look and bear witness, as did the poet, who had
been dispatched from Odessa to interview victims and report on
the events of violence in their aftermath. The poem that emerges
from the collected testimony is theatrical, even melodramatic, but
not without its realism. "And to the attics of the roofs you'll climb
and stand there in the darkness— / while bitter fear of death still
gnaws in lightless quiet." However belatedly, I am responding to
the poet's exhortation.

In many of the eyewitness accounts there are stories about
feathers flying (the quilts and mattresses were filled with them).
Korolenko vividly describes the scene at House No. 13, where two
of the already wounded were "finished off with crowbars, amidst
the derisive laughter of the onlookers, who covered the bodies
with feathers." Later on, rioters emptied casks of wine and "the
unfortunate victims were literally smothered in this mass of wine,
mud and feathers."

There is something strangely domestic, almost intimate
about this pogrom—the sense of a household being exposed.
Later, back in New York, looking at the pogrom images again and
thinking about the women's panic as they faced the violation of
their homes and bodies, I remembered a drama with feathers in
the tiny and chilly maid's room I rented in Paris, when I was a
graduate student. My grandmother's red taffeta quilt had moved

to France with me. I cannot reconstruct exactly how it was that the quilt—large, puffy, and entirely unlike the sturdy, blue Hudson Bay wool blankets we had grown up with—had somehow become mine. It might have been the only object that my father took from his mother's apartment after her death. Maybe it became mine because I was always cold.

One night, the quilt must have slipped off the narrow bed and onto the little electric space heater that I always kept next to me in the long Paris winter. The electrified feathers flew up like a snowstorm, blinding me for a moment. I was sure the whole room would catch on fire, but I managed to douse the smoldering quilt with cold water from my sink. The next morning, I packed up all the feathers I could gather in a bag and took it to a neighborhood mattress shop; restitched, the cover was still red, but the quilt itself had become a scaled-down version of its former, luxurious self. I found little feathers everywhere for ages. Now I think of the coverlet as an imaginary relic of the pogrom, a wounded remembrance, and I still wrap myself in its small square.

Who is to say that the feathers didn't travel from Kishinev to New York, when my grandparents left the city in 1906?

School 22 across the street, a functioning Jewish high school, is the next stop on the pilgrimage, and then the Gleizer Synagogue, the only operating synagogue in Kishinev. The synagogue, which has been carefully restored, appears to be a going concern, offering various community services. I'm not sure who supports this venue (everything seems funded, if underfunded, from abroad, the United States or Israel), but the name of the Joint Distribution Committee appears like a signature on the folding map of "Jewish Kishinev" that I will take home as a souvenir. Standing in the empty synagogue on a sunny Sunday morning, I am free to imagine that my grandparents attended services here, but the archives that might have contained their names no longer exist.

Walking between the school and the synagogue, I stare at, almost admire, since I'm partial to ruins, the crumbling skeleton of the former almshouse, remains of a world in which there were enough Jews to require such a splendid site of charity.

Tolstoy Street No. 23, with a bust of the great author affixed to the wall, Tolstoy who expressed his rage and horror over the events of the pogrom.

The monument linking the anniversary of the 1903 pogrom to the memory of Kishinev Jewish ghetto prisoners.

I snap pictures at each of our stops, my journey to what in this city, except for the monuments, my grandparents might have seen, belonged to, cared about. I re-create their missing album.

A Jewish Via Dolorosa.

I'm not searching for names on family graves in the large, overgrown cemetery, where the Torah scrolls, desecrated during the pogrom, have been reburied. My grandparents, presumably, left the city of the killings in order not to die there. I'm attached to this Jewish collective through the people, like my grandparents, who belong to the history of emigration, of departure. At the same time, because I am descended from their departure, I have the strange feeling of a lost home, almost as if they left in order for me to be able to return. But what, really, do I have in common with this nation, except for the long past history of emigration and the pogrom. Can my pogrom attachment survive the century of transformation?

The Jewish past of Kishinev is not only the pogrom and the dead buried in the cemetery. A small but vital community works to preserve Jewish history and bring it into the present of Chisinau both as memory and practice. Housed in the former mikveh of the former Woodcutter's Synagogue, the Jewish Museum is a one-room affair. The curator, Dorina, runs the little museum by herself. A collage of black-and-white photographs of the pogrom and of young men holding the desecrated Torah scrolls has been shaped around an arch against a painted backdrop of old Kishinev. As she describes the collection, the curator reviews local Moldovan history for me, especially the treatment of Jews during World War II, which is the primary focus of the objects in the vitrines. I listen intently, noting tiny bits of information in my diary. Standing there in the cold, I can't help conjuring up the naked women, maybe even my grandmother, who once engaged in their ritual baths here. Damp as it is in the museum, I've been unable to ignore the ghosts of female intimacies haunting the very foundations of archived history.

The library, where we go next, houses the Jewish Community Center and contains a small inventory of books, its authors identified by handwritten labels. There's also a pottery studio for children, a playroom, and a music studio. With my donation to the library, I acquire an album of Klezmer songs recorded by local musicians, and also a mezuzah, handmade and painted in bright colors (mine is turquoise) by the children who come to the center after school. There is something endearing but also wrenching to me about this microcosm of a living Jewish world, a miniature community, all contained within a single building.

The border between Moldova and Ukraine is marked by the river Dniester. The river at this point is not very wide, and you can see the people waiting on the other side. Natasha tells me the story of a man she took on a "roots trip" in this area, a man whose grandfather had been a ferryman. The grandson crossed the river at the exact spot where his grandfather had worked.

That is what I want and why I'm going to Ukraine: my analog of the memorial crossing, one hundred years later.

Natasha and I cross on the ferry alone because Slava, our driver, doesn't seem to have the right papers for taking a car across the border. He fails to persuade the customs guards to let him through, and they haul him off to the closest town to buy a new sticker. When Slava finally arrives in Ukraine, he drives at top speed on the two-lane highway so that we can still make our meeting in Vinnitsa, a small city about one hundred miles north of Chisinau. We have a rendezvous with an archivist Natasha has identified, who is waiting for us at the train station. The big open fields with huge, bright-yellow patches of rapeseed used for biofuel; horse-drawn carriages, piled high with hay; peasants working with hoes; clusters of wandering cows, it all looks just like the landscapes from the movie version of *Everything Is Illuminated*, even though the road scenes were shot in the Czech Republic. I sometimes have to remind myself that I've not wandered into a movie I've already seen.

At the outdoor café adjacent to the station, we discuss, over variants of borscht, the economics of the research I might be underwriting. The Ukrainian archivist, Vasily Morozov, is a balding, middle-aged man, who looks the part of a mid-level bureaucrat in an Eastern European film. Like Alla, Morozov freelances, but unlike Alla, who charges just an hourly rate, Morozov includes travel, lodging, and food in his fees because the Bratslav archives have been dispersed throughout the region, when they weren't destroyed during the war. In addition to those expenses, Morozov has (also unlike Alla) a $100 finder's fee. He distinguishes between "the thing itself," as he calls it—the coveted document; in my case, records of my grandparents' marriage or my uncle's birthplace—and "indirect," what he considers "side" information, for which he doesn't charge.

The archivist seems knowledgeable and gives us a tantalizing preview of the sorts of things he might look for. Still, as we talk, I start having cold feet. I will need to send cash to some poor woman in his village rather than to him because he doesn't want to pay taxes on the money I would transfer. Later, when we ask if we can call his home, where he has told us he has a daughter who speaks English, he says no, without explaining why. I hesitate, not only because these conditions make future transactions feel overly complicated but because the man himself seems both uneasy and cagey. It's possible that this impression is a function of the fact that the man never smiles, perhaps self-conscious about his teeth, most of which are missing; those that remain, I confess, have absorbed my attention, especially the single gold one at the top. It's also the case that the chances are not good for discoveries in this region, as the man himself has acknowledged. On the other hand, why go this far and stop? I still have so many gaps to fill in, the mysterious, dauntingly blank spaces between the points on my map.

Sitting at the café, I feel a spreading, almost physical thudding of embarrassment, of dismal reality seeping in, that threatens to erode the whole enterprise, my own belief in the quest itself.

Bratslav is one hour away on the Southern Bug, the river that flows through Vinnitsa. Despite my growing anxiety about the archivist, I'm excited about getting to the place where my grandfather Raphael and his father, my great-grandfather Chaim, were born. Here at least is something I can claim to know. Chaim left Bratslav for America in 1899, when he was forty-six. We pull up in front of a house with a hand-lettered sign advertising "European clothes" and ask the woman standing in the doorway how to get to the cemetery, which is the landmark for Bratslav. She tells us that the person we want to see is "Fima" and points us toward his house, a few streets away.

Fima, Ephraim Rabinovitch, born in 1948, appears to be the official Jewish face of the town. There are eight remaining Jews, he says, which may include his daughter, son-in-law, and granddaughter, who live with him. Fima is in charge of security at the cemetery, he tells us, and has in fact been featured in a video about the town, which Natasha and I are summoned to watch in the living room. Clearly we've come to the right place. When I ask, later, to take his picture, to which he gladly agrees, he retrieves a big, silver Jewish star, which has been stashed away in a drawer, and hangs it around his neck. Fima has a degree in biology, but judging by his track pants and bedroom slippers, he looks to be retired from his teaching job.

We have interrupted Fima's lunch, and so we sit down with him and Pavel, a Ukrainian from the town, whose parents, he tells us, belonged to a Christian religious sect called "Old Believers" and saved Jews during the Holocaust. His father worked in a power plant; his mother was a teacher. After the death of their parents, his brothers moved to Israel. It's not entirely clear why he has remained, or why his daughter, who had emigrated to Israel, returned to live with him.

Fima's grandparents would have been about ten years younger than mine, and so I am hoping he will have stories about Bratslav when my relatives lived here, but that does not interest him. Fima wants to talk about the Holocaust, in particular about the camp at Pechora (eleven miles east of Bratslav), the "Dead Loop," as it was known, where his parents were interned during the war. Fima is almost desperately eager to tell us about this camp, and he shows us literature on the subject, including a map of the area in which the camp was located. I did not know about the camps in Ukraine, and Fima's stories are both shocking in themselves and unexpected. At least 35,000 Jews were sent to Pechora; about 350 were still alive in the camp at the time of liberation, including his mother. At one point in his narrative, Fima recounts an episode of cannibalism in the camp during which a woman cut off her breast in order to provide food for her child. He describes the scene animatedly, then urges me to eat, serve myself from the table laden with food.

There are many, many graves in the Bratslav cemetery, high on the hill overlooking the River Bug. I have no idea where my great-grandfather's ancestors are buried, but even with no precise knowledge or individual connections, you can't help but feel the deep pull of a lost community. Fima points to a mound of rubble from an old synagogue. Natasha picks up some stones as a memento and I take a few pebbles as well.

The site only looks abandoned, though. On the hill sits the modern shrine the pilgrims come to honor in Bratslav: "Mausoleum of our teacher Rabbi Nathan." The prayer in Hebrew reads: "May his grace protect us, amen, disciple of our Rabbi Nachman of Bratzlav, may his grace protect us. Constructed by 'The Mausoleum of the Sages' by Rabbi Reb Israel Meir Gabbay, may the Lord give him life and strength." There's also another small building that's been designed to accommodate the pilgrims: "Hospitality. Bratslav. Built and taken care of by the Ohaley Tsadikim Committee [literally: the Tents of the Righteous, i.e., their tombs], directed by Rabbi Israel Meir Gabbay."

From the cemetery one can see the mill on the river, the picture-postcard image of Bratslav that appears on the Internet site and that I've photographed for myself, from what I hope is the same angle. If I've found nothing else, nothing like roots, it is at least gratifying to align my tourist's journey with the town's chosen icon. One half of the mill currently functions as a hydroelectric plant run by foreigners. The other half stands empty, and there is talk that some rich Israeli is going to convert it into a hotel for pilgrims. There's also an abandoned brick brewery of the same era that another foreigner, Fima says, may decide to renovate. There are few visible signs of modernization beyond those plans for the future, although many people, like Fima, have televisions sets. Perhaps, between the mill and the brewery, Bratslav will return to life, cycling back to the glories of its Hasidic past.

But I'm another kind of pilgrim, and ever since Fima's story about the "Dead Loop," I have been feeling almost stupidly persistent in wanting to find traces of the ordinary, everyday life that my great-grandparents would have had here. And so after the cemetery, we wander through a maze of deserted houses, set close together, almost hidden by trees and overgrown brush. One hundred years earlier in this rural village, the long, narrow, single-story houses were designed to accommodate large families. A waterman came around daily. Before emigration, my great-grandmother Sarah Kipnes, according to the Federal Census, had nine children in Bratslav, three of whom survived. Without an address or a photograph, there is no ancestral home, but why not imagine that my great-grandfather Chaim, the carpenter, had built houses like these, if not their roofs and floors? Visiting Bratslav is something like taking a tour of the Tenement Museum on the Lower East Side. I've entered the museum of the abandoned shtetl.

When I return to New York and send Fima snapshots from our afternoon and a cemetery donation, he sends me a copy of an old photograph I had admired in his living room, a panorama of the town's rooftops. I add this blurred, faded image of a lost landscape, dated from 1900—one year before my great-grandfather left Bratslav for America—to my repertoire of beloved views: the rooftops of Paris and the water towers of Manhattan. I now have in my possession the sloping, tiled, oblong roofs of the ancestral village.

I'm haunted by the document about the unnamed infant who lived for only three days, the child whose father, Refuel Kipnis, might have been from Tulchin. I remember Sarah's report that her father had made a notation in his last words to her about a baby spoon from Tulchin, possibly belonging to my grandfather's sister, Zirl. In 1900 the population of Bratslav was 3,900, Tulchin, 10,000. It would have made sense for the family to move to Tulchin for greater economic opportunities; maybe some of the family went on to Kishinev, or even Odessa. As we drive I try to figure out what connected the towns in this corner of Ukraine, and how my grandparents might have met. The railroad did not reach Bratslav, but the town was a great religious center; possibly my grandparents were introduced at one of the numerous local weddings. I mentally spin the story, but of course it's just that, spinning, like filling in the blanks between the dots, not enough to justify a visit. But we stop in Tulchin anyway, since it's a much larger town than Bratslav, where there is no restaurant, and we are all hungry.

As always, I'm hoping for a place that takes credit cards, because I am running out of cash and I know I have to pay Slava soon. I'm still annoyed with him for the delay he caused at the ferry crossing, which he persists in saying was not his fault: the papers worked before! I think he should give me a discount. I also don't have enough dollars or euros with which to pay his fee in the currencies he prefers. So I'm mad at Slava and I'm even madder at myself for not having brought more cash on the trip.

I argue loudly about the bill with Slava, who remains unmoved. He has his logic and his figures. And before I know it,
I'm sobbing in the empty restaurant. I cannot stop weeping. I'm
embarrassed to be crying in front of the driver; I'm mortified to
be crying over money. The whole trip is suddenly concentrated
in this moment of humiliation. Who am I, the woman weeping
in Tulchin? What am I weeping about? It was a mistake to go
alone. No wonder people would ask, worried and incredulous:
are you going alone? The truth is, I didn't have the right person to
go with. More tears about that. Then, finally, it's over. We figure
out the money, more or less, and we head out for the last stop
before the ferry back to Moldova, my grandmother's ancestral
village, Peschanka.

Months later I recognize that my breakdown in Tulchin was
not about underestimating how much cash to bring but about
everything that by definition I could not have calculated. Above
all, I had not expected to have the conversation with Fima in Bratslav. I had gone there with the mildest of expectations—I'd see
the village where my ancestors were born. I had not reckoned on
Fima's story about the Holocaust. I had not heard about camps in
Ukraine and I had not known that a camp had existed only miles
from Bratslav, the ancestral village I had only recently located
on a map. I had joked with friends whose families also came
from this area that, unlike our counterparts from Poland and
elsewhere, who hung around waiting for extinction, our brilliant
ancestors, like the inhabitants of Sholem Aleichem's stories, had
left town early. Because Fima was close to me in age, I realized
for the first time how close my own ancestors, starting with my
great-grandfather Chaim, could have come to elimination in the
Holocaust, had they remained. And so, in a way, the Holocaust
finally caught up with me.

Peschanka, my grandmother's birthplace. The cemetery, there's nothing else to visit, is tricky to get to, on a single-lane unpaved road. But when Slava pulls the car over to ask, everyone knows where it is—out of town, up a hill. Near the cemetery is a single, isolated house with a cross on the door. There are a few recently dated headstones at the edge of the burial ground, but it's impossible to escape the feeling that the cemetery's life, as it were, lies in the past. It's difficult to advance past the first few rows because the underbrush is thick and resistant. Still, we three go tramping around through the broken graves, pushing away the branches that hide their faded inscriptions—pointlessly, of course, since we lack the requisite linguistic knowledge—but we've made the journey and, therefore, we look.

I have photographed the town sign by the road, the place name that said Peschanka. It matches the name on my grandfather's first papers. But this is all I am going to know about these roots—the literal ones twisted tightly around the gravestones.

We still have to cross the Dniester again and return to Chisinau. It's 6:45 p.m. by the time we reach the border, but we are not worried: the day before, the friendly guard had said the last ferry was at 8 p.m. Slava gets out of the car to inquire, only to return almost immediately to say that there is no ferry. How can there be no ferry? The guard on duty explains that the ferry service is private, not governmental. It belongs to someone who lives on the Moldova side. The Moldovan owner has gotten bored waiting for cars to turn up, so he has decided to pack it in and go home.

We are all three incredulous, indignant. A young man comes by on his bike and laughs at our distress. "Where do you think you are," he asks scornfully, looking at Slava's Volkswagen Passat. "In Europe?" The next crossing of the river available to us is a bridge to the north. We have to drive back as far as Mogilyov Podolsk on the Ukraine side of the border. This will add 150 kilometers to our trip; what would have taken three hours will now take at least six. This is what it's like here, Natasha observes philosophically. This is why some people miss Communism; at least everything functioned.

We climb back into the car. Slava drops me off at the Hotel Dacia at midnight. I give him all the local currency in my possession as a tip for the extra hours. It's the least I can do to paper over my tantrum in Tulchin.

The roots adventure began with a photograph—the photograph of my grandparents and my uncle taken in Kishinev circa 1903. On my last day in 2008 Chisinau, Natasha and I set out to look for the street on which we believe the photography studio had once been located, and we arrive at the place whose name had changed four times with the different political regimes: Kharlampievska Str., at the time of the photo, 1903; Str. 27 March 1918 in Romanian time, 1918–40; in Soviet time, 1989, Str. Stefan Veliky, Stephen the Great; and now, since independence, Alexandru Cel Bun. This pretty, leafy area was not situated in the path of the pogrom but in the central part of the city, on the fringes of respectability. A travel shop and a bridal shop occupy the ground floor of the building. What do you know when you stand on the location, what *might be* the location? I snap the picture all the same.

Natasha and I walk around the back of the building that supposedly housed the photography studio (the building is now painted purple), to see whether anyone remembers the studio. In the courtyard we see that a few families remain; most have left for Israel or the United States. I conjure up the ghosts of a petit-bourgeois family coming to have its picture taken here, more than one hundred years ago, worried about pogroms and hoping to leave for America. (All the while, I'm taking mental notes for a talk I'm scheduled to give in Antwerp a few days later: "My Kishinev Pogrom: An American Story.")

With the photography studio identified, as we have chosen to believe, I am free to enjoy the streets of Chisinau without a pogrom head. I actually want to mail a postcard, like a tourist, and I can do this only from the post office. For the first time, I see the more familiar, Western European turn of twentieth-century architecture and well-laid-out, tree-lined streets, different from the scrambled lanes of the pogrom zone and the hulks of aging Soviet construction. Fleetingly, I imagine my stylishly dressed grandparents strolling past these graceful *pierre de taille* buildings, including the court where the pogrom trial was held, dreaming of America under the shade of the chestnut trees.

Natasha and I stop at the post office and make our way into a little crowded park, where crafts and household objects are arrayed for sale. She helps me select a Russian Matryoshka doll for my new little Miller godchild, my cousin's granddaughter, back in New York. I probably could have purchased the same set of colorfully painted, egg-like nested dolls from a stand in front of the Metropolitan Museum of Art, but I, at least (she is much too young to care), will always know that this particular one is a real souvenir from a place that is no more.

13. The Silverware from Russia

Just as the purely patrilineal Old Testament genealogies leave out the mothers and even the fathers of the mothers, so these tidy stories leave out all the sources and inspirations that come from other media and other encounters, from poems, dreams, politics, doubts, a childhood experience, a sense of place, leave out the fact that history is made more of crossroads, branchings, and tangles than straight lines. These other sources I called the grandmothers. | Rebecca Solnit, *A Field Guide to Getting Lost*

There was one exception to the rule of silence in family matters. The silverware from Russia.

In the 1980s, a few years after my mother's death, my father presented me with three forks and three spoons. Simple in design and bent from years of wear, the heavy silver forks and spoons seemed oversized for an ordinary table setting. They resembled serving pieces, and some were engraved with monograms. All were stamped on the back with the silvermark and with dates—1873 and 1879—and tiny indented icons, one of which appears to be a miniature castle. I don't remember my father's saying more than that the silverware had belonged to his family, "our family," as he put it, which I assumed—as I typically did with all the objects of my inheritance—meant that the forks and spoons came from the Kipnises, from his father's side. I also assumed that the monogrammed initials would reflect that line of descent, but since the letters were in Cyrillic, it wasn't immediately obvious. Several years later, during an office hour, when I was not yet fully embarked on the quest, I asked one of my students, who was studying Russian, what the letters translated to in English. "N and SH," she said, after examining the photocopy I had made. Expecting her to say "K" for Kipnis, I was baffled. Who was SH and who was N?

Yet another enigma, this time from the kitchen drawer.

During the years of the quest, before I knew I wanted to write a book about the recovery of my lost family, or knew what kind of story it would be, long periods of a kind of peculiar lethargy alternated with sudden bursts of activity. In one of those sporadic efforts to gather momentum and connect to the few real people who remained alive, I decided to telephone my father's relatives in Canada, to see what more they could tell me about Dvorah, their mother's (and my grandmother's) sister, the woman whose existence had been revealed in the letter from Argentina.

It embarrasses me to call people I know only slightly, even if we are related, to ask them to take part in my undertaking. While theoretically shareable with them—after all, it was as much *their* family as mine—the effort seemed driven by my own concerns: a preoccupation with the past I barely understood myself and a book I was writing. It was as though I were asking strangers to indulge me, to humor this odd, distant cousin at the other end of the line.

I was first worried about Gert, the cousin I knew better because I had stayed in her apartment on a visit to Montreal in the 1990s, and we had talked long into the night. I reached her son's wife, Nina, a Russian immigrant, who like me seemed to have taken on the role of family archivist. Nina told me that both sisters had died; I was mortified to be learning of their death only because I was selfishly pursuing my roots-seeking obsession. Why had I waited so long? Perhaps I preferred living with mystery to living with disappointment (maybe they wouldn't know anything), and perhaps in matters of biography and autobiography belatedness is the writer's inevitable position.

Nina knew the approximate date of my great-aunt Sarah's death, and she had heard from her mother-in-law, she said, that the parents of the three sisters had owned a brewery in Russia. She had the impression that the family belonged to an elite. She thought that Gert had started a memoir, but she didn't know what had come of it. In one of her letters to me after our time together in Montreal, which I remembered only after this conversation, Gert lamented her failing vision and her inability to find the energy to write a book about her family, as I had encouraged her to do over tea. "I think about how good it would be for my children to eventually get to know something about my roots, but for me," she wrote, "it is too late." My cousin's sadness about not telling that story makes me long to overcome her feeling of belatedness, moves me to counter that silence after the fact by following the traces of the unwritten history—like the story of our cousin in

Argentina, her gift to me. In the chain of indebtedness at the heart of family, I owe her that effort.

But what does it mean for me to write about my family's roots when I have no children who want to know their story? It means writing without the memoirist's alibi.

So I called my cousin Sam, Gert's nephew, the older of Fredi's two sons, the nephew whom I had once met when he made a trip to New York in the late 1950s. He remembered shocking my parents by saying he liked Ike, or was it Nixon? Neither of us was sure. While Sam and I were chatting, I was leafing through the cache of letters I had saved from the Canadian cousins to check on whether I had missed anything else about the family that he might be interested in seeing. I opened an envelope addressed to my father from his mother, dated 1985. "Thank you for the cutlery," Fredi wrote on the inside of a Hallmark card, "It is a great memento from our grandparents. I plan to divide it between Sholem [as they called Sam] and Nathan. I hope that eventually they will pass it on to their sons. I hope they will value it—remembering that it belonged to their great, great grandparents."

Staring at me, embedded in the thank-you note, was the origin of the family silver. The Cyrillic letter sounding "SH" would be Scholnick, the family name of the three sisters Sadie, Sarah, and Dvorah. But "N," could this be the unknown ancestor after whom I was named? I read my cousin his mother's note aloud and asked him whether he had received the silverware from his mother, or whether in emptying his mother's apartment he had found any of the pieces. He said he would look and that he thought there might be something among his mother's affairs that would interest me; he still hasn't gotten back to me—and I, equally remiss, have never sent him his mother's letter, as I intended to do. The card brought me information that the conversation itself failed to provide. But I might never have opened the little note card and read the message had I not forced myself to make the call.

In retrieving the past, there is no straight line.

As I was painfully learning, the knowledge I hungered for often came by chance; but without one's taking a first step, the accident could not happen. I had to set something in motion, set down the path, pick up the phone. Later that day, as I sifted through everything I had learned since speaking to my cousins in Canada, I checked the date of Fredi's note against my father's diary from 1985 to see whether my father mentioned giving his cousins the silverware, as he had noted the previous year that he had given the silverware to me. Tuesday, November 20, 1984: "Nance stopped by for a bite of lunch. I told her of the provenance of our silverware. She took some home plus some platters for Thanksgiving dinner on Thursday." Our silverware. He must have given a few pieces to Gert, when she visited my father in New York the following year. My hunch was correct, though as usual, nothing was quite as exact as one might have wished.

The diary records a phone call from Gert saying that she and her husband would *not* be visiting as planned. But then, tucked between the diary pages, one week later is a handwritten note from her saying how much she had enjoyed meeting my sister and me, and thanking my father for the "forks and knives that had belonged to our grandparents." She added that she had shared the silverware with her sister, who said she "would most probably give them to her younger son, Nathan." (I wondered whom Nathan had been named after—whose N?) The silverware wasn't all my father gave his cousin on her unrecorded visit. He also gave her a collection of Sholem Aleichem stories. Perhaps he connected the silverware to the fiction in order to put their shared objects into their shared lost story, making both more real.

I worried about the discrepancy in the diary and about my reliance on it as a kind of truth, when clearly—or not so clearly—my father's mind was working only intermittently. I wanted everything in the diary to be true. I wanted to have access to the record of my father's inner life. Still, what choice did I have but to rely on the unreliable? Besides, with a story whose pieces were like the silverware—stamped with history but largely mute—I had to realize that I could go only so far and no farther—without my own embellishments. So my father's mother Sheyndel, I decided, was the first of the three sisters to leave Russia for the West. Probably the oldest of the three, she took all the family silver on her journey, which my father ultimately shared with her sisters' children, fifty years after her death—and with me. I'm keeping the silver for now, although I have already given a fork and spoon to my goddaughter, who shares Eastern European roots through her maternal grandmother; the remainder I plan to leave to Sarah, for her family. In the meantime, I use the silverware every day, as a kind of practice in memory.

Not long after my conversation with my cousin in Canada, when I traveled to Kishinev, I carried one of the monogrammed pieces with me in my suitcase. I asked my guide Natasha to decipher the initials on the handle. She immediately read the mark of the family name as "SH," but she read the first initial in Cyrillic not as "N" but as the English sound "JU," as in Julia, or my maternal great-grandfather's name, Judah.

The objects bearing the traces of my Russian origins belonged to the Scholnick family tree, bringing me back once more, against my expectations, to my grandmother's side of the silenced stories.

14. My Grandmother's Dunams

He walked back along Dorset street, reading gravely. Agendath Netaim: planter's company. To purchase vast sandy tracts from Turkish government and plant with eucalyptus trees. Excellent for shade, fuel and construction. Orangegroves and immense melonfields north of Jaffa. You pay eighty marks and they plant a dunam of land for you with olives, oranges, almonds or citrons. | James Joyce, *Ulysses*

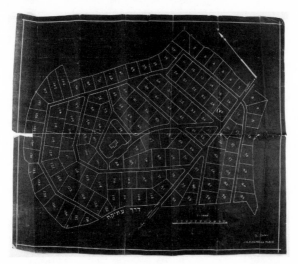

Would I have ever come to tell this story if my grandmother had not bought two dunams of land in British Mandate Palestine from Yitzhaq Feller in 1926, when he toured the synagogues on the

Lower East Side looking for clients? Actually, this tiny plot of land, the equivalent of one half acre, was paid for by my grandfather. He signed the checks, but the certificate of ownership was issued in my grandmother's name, and her initials appear on the map of the property. I'm still not sure what to make of this arrangement—whether my grandfather feared he would die soon (as he did eight years after paying the last installment on the land) and wanted his future widow to have an investment, whether this was a convention in Jewish families, or whether it was my grandmother's idea, from the era when she was the "boss" to my grandfather's *nudnik*. Feller's brochure pitched the Mizrachi Zionist fantasy with rhetorical brio: "If you want the Holy Land redeemed . . . If you want your name inscribed in Jewish History, as one who helped build the Holy Land . . . If you want to strengthen the spirit of Judaism—Buy a dunam of land in Nachlas Itzchak, near Jerusalem." I guess they wanted all that, and so they signed on.

In the late 1990s, during a brief stay in Israel, I met a young scholar, Tamar Hess, who shared my fascination with family stories. We had remained in touch over the years, and on a more recent visit to the country, as we drove to the airport, I happened to tell her about my grandmother's property as an amusing, bittersweet story—almost as a curious footnote, another installment of family enigmas now behind me. Nonetheless, when I returned to New York I forwarded her all the documentation in my possession, including a narrative composed by the researcher who had first unearthed our family claim in the Israeli archives. The researcher detailed the lengthy process that had ended with the sale of the land to a Jewish religious broker from Jerusalem for a sum half of which the property had originally been assessed for in the courts, and well below half of the figure that had been floated at the beginning of the entire process at the time of the phone call in 2000. Although the four-page, single-spaced real estate saga was somewhat bewildering because of the intricacies governing property transactions in Israel, the bottom line, when it emerged from the thicket of bureaucratic prose, was clear enough: the sale of the property had been disappointing. "We invested a great amount of time and effort for minimal returns," was the conclusion, blunt and to the point.

Tamar answered almost immediately: "This is quite uncanny. This plot is one of the saddest and most famous real estate fiascos in the Jerusalem area in the last few years." And she proceeded to flesh out the story. The government had designated the area in the Jerusalem Hills known as Ein Hemed—*ein*, Hebrew for spring or source of water, *hemed*, Hebrew for beauty or charm—as a natural resource area. Although Ein Hemed—a beautiful hilltop setting overlooking the Jerusalem–Tel Aviv road—was meant to be a nature reserve, the government's master plan allowed for the building of a hotel (requiring twenty dunams) to encourage tourism, but not for small, individual properties. A developer thought he could circumvent the restrictions by an act of wishful interpretation, building individual houses and calling them "holiday apartments." He sold them as such, hoping to tiptoe around the law without anyone noticing, and the new owners went ahead and obtained mortgages on the force of his convictions. But a whistle-blower brought the violation to the government's attention, and in 2002 the Supreme Court ruled that despite the acknowledged hardship to the buyers, the houses could not be occupied. Electricity and water were cut off. "The houses," Tamar wrote, "have stood there abandoned ever since. They cannot be lived in, and they are not being demolished. It's a ghost neighborhood. The reason I am aware of them is that they are about half a kilometer from where

I live. I drive past them several times a day. Their vacancy is very present in our local landscape." In the space of a month I had gone from having only the vaguest idea of where the property was located to having a friend who lived five minutes away from it. "Your plot," Tamar concluded, "might be the only part that was actually sold and that was not seized by the state."

Minimal returns. I weighed my friend's narrative against the real estate accounting. How bad, really, was the outcome, compared to no sale at all? Taking the long view, and looking at the property simply as a financial investment, the return on the purchase of the dunams had been relatively, if modestly, respectable—a rate of approximately 5 percent per annum between 1926 and 2006, the equivalent of an investment in conservative government bonds compounded annually. From a strictly monetary vantage point, the grandparents had done all right by their heirs. The chagrin about the final settlement was tied more to the roller-coaster of glorious expectations that had been set in motion by the initial phone call than by the actual sums of money disbursed.

I started to feel that the financial measure of "minimal returns" was precisely the wrong way to look on this inheritance. Just as my grandparents probably imagined their dunams as an emotional engagement with a vision they never expected to see as a concrete reality in their lifetime, my own investment in the sale of the property was also bound up with an idea. Not a messianic Zionism but rather a much smaller idea of these hardworking immigrants to whom I was related, as they negotiated their family's future in the crowded Jewish world of the Lower East Side.

My grandmother's dunams returned me to the couple who in 1926 decided to risk something in return for a feeling of community, to their story, in which I am now forever entangled.

I could not quite put the story to rest. I had unfinished business with the dunams that I had fantasized about for over five years. My grandparents had, no doubt, been satisfied to see their individual plot marked in red on the map. But I wanted to see the property—the ultimate object from the drawer—for myself. Despite the photographs and the documentation, the half-acre suburban equivalent I had conjured up did not bring me close enough to the thing itself. I felt compelled to stand on the land, on the plot my grandparents had funded, grounding their gesture.

Tamar met me at the airport. As soon as I dropped my bags at her house, she drove us to see what I kept calling "my property," even though it had been sold and had never been entirely mine. Within minutes, we pulled up on the edge of the road, where the sign said, in Hebrew, Ein Hemed in large letters, and in small, Rehov Nahalt Yitzchak. By this time, having pored over the documents so compulsively, I could almost decipher the Hebrew letters.

We wandered through the stretch of deserted houses, taking pictures and marveling that the government had actually forced the project to a halt. We wondered where exactly my dunams were, something we would only learn the next day, when the real estate researcher came to show us the exact location. As it turned out, our dunams were elsewhere, in an area slightly below the abandoned compound, closer to the road, on land that had not been developed. The land itself was scruffy, but it was not difficult to imagine how the lot might be landscaped, taking advantage of the local trees—carob, almond, olive—and the spectacular view.

Standing there and thinking about how much blood had been shed nearby in what was called "the butcher's arena" in 1948, I couldn't feel sorry that we were no longer absentee foreign owners. It made a kind of sense that the actual buyer and current dunam owner, Mr. Eli Cohen, of Jerusalem, could take the long, possibly messianic perspective that someday the government would have to change its mind and allow for development, and that he would then be sitting on a quite desirable piece of property, just as we had thought in the beginning. In theory, this is a decision that, as heirs, we could have taken: wait and see. Why sell for so little money? But we heirs were growing old and not living with biblical temporalities.

By the time the estate was settled in 2006, Julian had died and left everything to his second wife, thereby excluding his daughter, Sarah, from the inheritance. I had become attached to Sarah and was shocked at the exclusion that, to my mind, broke the genealogical chain connecting us all. For my part, as the years went by and the prospects of success seemed more and more remote, I had begun to look on the financial outcome as if not irrelevant to the story the legacy had generated, at least quite secondary to it. I became instead more and more invested in all that the possibility of the inheritance had opened up to my imagination. In addition to the people I had met for the first time, to whom I was more or less distantly related—Julian and Sarah, Sarah's family, then my ninety-seven-year-old cousin in Tucson, Brownie, and her daughter, Sarah—there were also the family members I had discovered through documents and photographs, who also belonged to the history out of which I had emerged: my uncle Sam, my grandfather's siblings—my great-aunt and great-uncle, my grandmother's sister in Argentina, my cousins in Canada. I had entered a new world of relation.

As I slowly collect the fragments of my grandmother's biography, both the gestures of her life like the purchase of the dunams and the objects related to her existence within the family—the letter from her sister in Argentina, the silverware with her father's initials, the red taffeta quilt—I'm moved to see that without her there would be no story. Without her nieces—whom I knew and thought of as my father's cousins—I would never have found the key to that side of the family, the *other side of the other side*. I did not go looking for her, the one Kipnis relative I had in fact known, if only from childhood. On the contrary, and even perversely, I overlooked her at almost every turn as I unconsciously repeated the act of excluding her from the disappeared family I was trying to trace, just as she had been excluded from our ordinary family life in New York.

My grandmother was always a shadowy figure dressed in black with an embroidered white-lace collar, I'm tempted to say a powdery figure. If I try to capture her now in memory, I can almost smell a faint odor of dusting powder of the kind that no one uses anymore, but I cannot remember a word she said. There are very few photographs of her with any of us: one with my mother, around the time of my parents' marriage in the 1930s, the one in Riverside Park, where she stood alone but smiling as she held me when I was a newborn, and one of her seated, stiff and lonely, at a Miller Seder table. She was missing from the family albums as she had been missing from our lives.

But now I've placed her above my desk, preening on the wall, in a very large framed image, looking proud and somehow Victorian in a portrait taken at the Randell Studio, 57 Avenue B, New York. The portrait never hung in my parents' apartment; I found it hidden away, deep in one of the bedroom closets. I suppose that my mother did not relish a prominent visual reminder of the woman she found so difficult. For my part, my grandmother makes more sense to me fixed in this photograph than she ever did alive, when I was a child bewildered by her foreignness and isolation. Bedecked and bejeweled, her short, stout figure enfolded in an elaborately draped dress, her arms posed to show off sheer, embroidered-lace sleeves, Sadie, still Sheyndel to intimates, is heading out, I've decided, undaunted, for Maurice Schwartz's Yiddish Art Theatre to enjoy the fundraiser of Sholem Aleichem's *Stempenyu*, ready to face the richer wives of her husband's Talmud Torah. I can't help feeling sad that I missed this part of her—a woman with unforgiving standards and total clarity about what she wanted from the world, including her dresses, but I am consoled to have found her so many years later. I have restored her posthumously to a place of benevolence, only to lose her again. *Zie gezunt*, as my father used to say by way of farewell, be well.

15. Family Hair Looms

What was her story? The worst of it is I am not sure. No matter how poignant the details, the narrative is pieced together by something which by itself may be a distortion: my own wish to make something orderly out of these fragments. To transpose them from a text where the names were missing or erased to one where they were clear. | Eavan Boland, *Object Lessons*

The hair had been saved in a crumbling cardboard box that once contained scented French soap. When I first raised the lid of the box tucked away in a corner of my father's dresser drawer, I was sure that the fair, tightly curled hair was payess, the long side locks worn by Jewish ultra-orthodox and Hasidic men. I eyed the curls suspiciously and with a certain visceral anxiety, alternately attracted and repelled by the object. Whose hair was this? Not my father's, whose hair, like mine, dark and tightly kinked, could never have been smoothed into that pale cylindrical shape. My grandfather's, then? From the black-and-white photographs I could not tell what kind of hair he had, though it looked thin and straight enough to have been twirled this fine. Who had kept the locks and why?

Despite the lack of any information about the previous owner of the hair—the head to which the hair originally belonged—it felt as though I had become a belated witness to a familial act of

severance. A male relative on the Kipnis side (on my mother's side, everyone had bone-straight black hair), I fantasized, had cut off his payess in a gesture of rebellion against the ancient observance. But this was just a feeling. Was it even a custom to preserve severed payess?

I asked Susannah Heschel, a well-known scholar of Jewish history and religious practice, for her view of the payess hypothesis. "In the Jewish tradition," she explained, "hair is supposed to be burned, not preserved." But then she went on to consider my problem midrashically, I'm tempted to say. Someone untraditional enough to cut off his payess would not worry about burning it. "Who saved the payess?" she wondered rhetorically. "Presumably his wife, perhaps as a nostalgic remembrance of the old ways together, the commitment to Orthodoxy, perhaps the wedding of two young people from religious homes, now repudiated—though not without some sadness." This interpretation made a certain sense, given what I know about my family. Perhaps my grandfather Rafael rebelled against his pious father by leaving his natal Hasidic village of Bratslav with his new bride, Sheyndel, cutting off the signs of his religious observance the better to mark off a past life. Since, as the photographs show, my grandfather had already trimmed his beard in Russia, and then shaved it entirely when he got to America, this story feels plausible.

At the same time, although the payess-cutting scenario was seductive, I also briefly entertained the notion that the curls belonged to a boy, a son, possibly my little uncle Sam, whose hair, according to ultra-orthodox Jewish tradition, would have been cut for the first time at age three in a formal ceremony. In this ritual haircut that corresponds to the festival Lag Ba'Omer, boys are shorn of the hair on their head, except for the ear locks, which by contrast attain prominence.

Unfortunately, with this box of curls, there was just too much hair for a three-year-old child. And probably too much for payess, as well, despite the highly suggestive evidence I saw as I walked through the streets of New York, and later Jerusalem, where I identified many candidates for the thickly rolled specimens resting in the Savon Violette box.

The payess hypothesis was dealt a serious blow when I showed the actual locks—not just the photograph of them—to another scholar of Jewish history and culture, Barbara Kirshenblatt-Gimblett. She took the view that the curls had belonged to a woman, an Orthodox woman, she reasoned, whose hair was sacrificed before marriage in preparation for wearing a wig. After inspecting my heirloom, my Judaica expert forwarded the following account of a bridal hair-cutting posted on an Internet site:

The next morning after the khupah *[ceremony], when the* sheitl *[wig] had already been sent to the bride at home, the regal* siddur *[prayer book] in the golden cloth with a lock, a* shkot *(a mirror in a [wooden] frame), etc, according to one's financial ability, the groom's mother, often with all of the relatives went to see the* nakhas *[proud enjoyment], that is, if the mitzvah was done in the true Jewish way, and the bride was lifted from the bed. After undressing her, her hair was cut, during which the young, often 14 or 15-year-old bride heartbreakingly would cry over her beautiful cut locks and braids. After the cutting, the bride would be veiled.*

Kirshenblatt-Gimblett reflected on this third possibility of a woman's nostalgia for her youthful self, citing the example of her own family as possible evidence: "Who knows? Longing for the shorn locks? Especially in later periods when girls may have not wanted to go along with this anyway (my father's mother, for example)." Maybe my grandmother had saved her own maidenly curls, even though she did not, even in the earliest photographs, wear a wig or cover her hair.

How to decide? A young man saving the proof of his rebellion? A father saving locks from his son's first ritual haircut? A young woman's sacrifice to tradition before her own marriage? Even DNA analysis would not resolve the conundrum my locks presented, since, according to the science, without a follicle, without a root, gender cannot be determined.

But what if Jewish tradition had nothing to do with it? What if my grandmother—assuming for the sake of argument that the saver was my grandmother, a woman fond of fashion—one day simply decided to abandon her locks in favor of a new style? Or what if, when her husband unexpectedly died and she was newly widowed, my grandmother decided that curls no longer suited her, mourned her loss through the cut, and saved the hair in remembrance of the marital bond?

As a result of telling Tamar's friends in Israel about my hair problem, still another expert in Judaica, Lester Vogel, wrote to me about a comparable object belonging to his family. He remembered seeing hair preserved under glass in a picture frame, only to discover, when he looked, that "the hair had been removed." At some point in the picture's history, "the hair had been taken out and placed in a separate small, common brown bag," after which it disappeared. What intrigued me in the story was my correspondent's hypothesis that the vanished curls belonged to his mother-in-law when she was a girl, and that they would have been cut off at about the time she went to public school.

This image of a seven-year-old girl on her way to school sent me back to a photograph of my father's Canadian cousins. In addition to the two cousins I knew, I had heard of a third sister, a sister who died young and whose name I never learned. I suddenly found myself wondering whether the little girl in the family picture, taken at the time of my father's visit to Montreal with his mother in the summer of 1934, the little girl almost out of the frame, with her head tilting under the weight of her long sausage curls, wasn't the daughter of this woman, and by that relation, a great-niece of my grandmother's. Women of earlier eras often saved hair from children and lovers in scrapbooks and albums. Maybe, I've begun to think, the unnamed great-niece is, in the end, the likeliest candidate of them all.

Unlike a letter, hair is unsigned, and as family hair it looms large in my imagination. The locks are links in a chain that binds me tightly to the past, even if I can't fully decipher either hair or past. As the final keeper of the locks, I can bring them into language, into the world of lost stories within which they once held meaning.

There is, for instance, a well-known Hasidic story that goes like this:

When the Baal Shem had a difficult task before him, he would go to a certain place in the woods, light a fire and meditate in prayer—and what he had set out to perform was done. When a generation later the "Maggid" of Meseritz was faced with the same task he would go to the same place in the woods and say: We can no longer light the fire, but we can still speak the prayers—and what he wanted done became reality. Again a generation later Rabbi Moshe Leib of Sassov had to perform this task. And he too went into the woods and said: We can no longer light a fire, nor do we know the secret meditations belonging to the prayer, but we do know the place in the woods to which it all belongs—and that must be sufficient; and sufficient it was. But when another generation had passed and Rabbi Israel of Rishin was called upon to perform the task, he sat down on his golden chair in his castle and said: We cannot light the fire, we cannot speak the prayers, we do not know the place, but we can tell the story of how it was done. And, the storyteller adds, the story he told had the same effect as the actions of the other three.

As the great-granddaughter of a man born in the town of Bratslav, a town still famous because of the Hasidic writer who once lived there, I feel tempted to read the story autobiographically. I see in the story of the generation that went to the woods, that returned to the woods, and that emerged never to return again except in memory, and even then at several removes, the outlines of a familiar pattern. My great-grandparents and my grandparents said the prayers, lit the candles, and believed in their community. My grandfather loved, longed for, lived for his Talmud Torah on the Lower East Side, and he wrote letters in Yiddish. What happened after that, to the generations of my family that no longer said the prayers or lit the candles, is the story embedded in this book, a story about forgetting traditions. But the fable also suggests that despite the losses something remains: the power of reciting "the story of how it was done."

If to honor the generations that came before me, and that I now know to be mine, I remember occasionally to light a candle, if I am a Jew only through the imagination of history, a history that includes the woods, I am also the storyteller of that journey. In the end, what binds me intimately to this narrative is not the belief of faith, which is not mine, but the belief that what matters is the effort entailed in coming to know when, if not why, the stories stopped.

I share my grandmother's taste for scented French soap, but that doesn't completely explain my obsession with this strange memory object. Metaphorically, at least, I seem to want to reattach myself to a tradition from which I had, for a long time, chosen to sever myself, or at least to re-create a connection to a narrative that had long been lost to me.

16. Return to Kishinev

We are beguiled. It happens mostly in our old age, when our personal futures close down and we cannot imagine—sometimes cannot believe in—the future of our children's children. We can't resist this rifling around in the past, sifting the untrustworthy evidence, linking stray names and questionable dates and anecdotes together, hanging on to threads, insisting on being joined to dead people and therefore to life. | Alice Munro, *The View from Castle Rock*

Less than a year after my first and, I thought surely, my once-in-a-lifetime roots trip to the city of Kishinev, I found myself planning a return engagement. I had already walked the streets that the *pogromchiks* had followed. I had gone to the old cemetery and contemplated the crumbling gravestones that marked the lives of Jews long dead. I had located what might have been the building that housed the photography studio where my grandparents had had their picture taken. I had seen what "Jewish Kishinev" had to offer. Why, then, did I decide to return? Was it only because, as Munro suggests, the lives of the dead are paradoxically enlivening, and I needed another jolt of something from the past that would bring me more securely into the future?

Two unrelated incidents converged to precipitate the second pilgrimage: the publication of Aleksandar Hemon's novel, *The*

Lazarus Project, and the discovery of a strange album of photographs belonging to my grandmother. Together, these two new objects, the novel and the album, compelled the return to Kishinev in the summer of 2009.

Lazarus Averbach is a survivor of the 1903 Kishinev pogrom who emigrates to the safety of America only to be murdered a few years later in Chicago. Brik, the narrator, and his travel companion, Rora, a photographer, head for Kishinev to find out what happened to the victim: "The two of us who could never have experienced the pogrom went to the Chisinau Jewish Community Center to find someone who had never experienced it and would tell us about it." I read the novel with a sense of growing anxiety. Here was my own private adventure, which I had thought daring and original (let others go to Polish shtetls), somehow scooped and transformed into literature through an artful postmodern scrim. Naturally, their guide resembles a Philip Rothian character, a beautiful, if slightly bored young woman, pale with "deep, mournful eyes."

The beautiful guide dutifully recounts the events of 1903 before showing the two men to an adjacent room, where they gaze in horror at a display of photographs: "bearded, mauled corpses lined up on the hospital floor, the glassy eyes facing the ceiling stiffly; a pile of battered bodies; a child with its mouth agape; a throng of bandaged, terrified survivors." I recognized the terrible images of the pogrom victims, but I had not seen them on my visit. Could I have seen them and forgotten?

Insidiously, Hemon's fiction began to undermine my sense of reality. In the novel, for instance, the two characters quickly leave the display of pogrom photographs and move further into the room. Behind an alcove they see "a couple of dummies in Orthodox Jewish attire, positioned around an empty table, their eyes wide open, their hands resting on the table's edge." Jewish dummies? I traveled back in my mind, racing through the pictures I had taken. No dummies. I sent Natasha, my guide, a frantic message, telling her about the novel and asking whether we had seen these rooms. Could we have missed the pogrom exhibit? Surely I would have noticed these "dummies." Natasha replied immediately, forwarding pictures from our time at the Jewish Library, including one of me looking at two elaborately costumed puppets. "Please see yourself with the puppets." But these puppets were Purim figures, Queen Esther and King Ahashuerus, not dummies dressed as Orthodox Jews. Had Hemon and I come to the same place?

Why is it so hard to stay present, to see what is there before one's eyes?

Unnerved by the novel, I started to distrust my reliability as the narrator of my memoir. I wrote to Olga, since the library was her domain, sharing the photographs now in my possession and laying out my confusion. "Aleksandar Hemon is correct in his description," Olga began. I held my breath, stunned by her confirmation of my memory lapse. She detailed "the reconstructed scene" of Jewish family life at the turn of the twentieth century. What about the dummies? "The dummies in Orthodox attire just symbolized the atmosphere of an average Jewish home." Finally, Olga explained that before 2005—presumably when Hemon had visited the city—the museum and, therefore, the exhibit were located across the street in another venue: "So you couldn't have seen the described artifacts." I had missed not only the scene with the dummies but also, Olga added, the "exposition devoted to Pogrom with a map, names of the victims, and a large picture of Torah scrolls damaged by the looters." My heart exploded with relief; I couldn't have seen what I didn't see!

Hemon's novel alternately punished and rewarded me. His

fiction revealed the fragility of my truth, but his story, along with the photographs I now had from the exhibit he had probably toured, helped me understand the interweaving of several threads in the reconstruction of Jewish memory in Moldova. On the banner floating above the photographs of the pogrom, lines in Soviet Yiddish orthography signed with Bialik's name and flanked by graphics depicting stylized figures consumed by grief call out prophetically: "Voices lament / By way of ancient rivers / Why why and again, why?" On a separate placard, also in Yiddish, the curators join historical events to the victims of Holocaust persecution: "This exhibition at the Jewish Museum was prepared by Izrail Pilat. It depicts Bessarabian Jewish martyrs from the Nazi occupation and serves as a memorial to his brother Sholem Pilat, the Zionist, who tragically perished in the ghetto." As I strained to connect the images from an exhibit I hadn't seen to the pages of the novel I had read, my effort to fathom the city's past felt like a replay of childhood trips to the Museum of Natural History, where we were instructed to gaze at dioramas of lost worlds and foreign peoples.

On my first trip to Kishinev I had arrived clutching the one photograph of my grandparents as the evidence of their connection to the city, and I had talked with Olga about photography studios. In 1918, she said, following up with me in an e-mail, there were ten photography studios in Kishinev, all of them owned and operated by Jews; she even had their names and addresses. When I expressed my surprise about the presence of so many Jews in this profession, Olga corrected me: "There is nothing strange in such popularity of the business among Jews, as they used to be pioneers in all progressive enterprises. Basically, Jews in Bessarabia started a lot of new industries." I was startled by this portrait of Jews as pioneers, as agents of modernity. But Olga's documentation fleshed out Alla's archival notation, *meshchanin*. I had not yet begun to consider the existence of class distinctions among Kishinev Jews. "Your family, if your grandfather was a bookkeeper," Olga explained, "belonged to the middle class of Bessarabian Jewry."

In our correspondence between the visits, Olga added facts about social and cultural life almost impossible for a non-specialist to uncover: "According to the general census of the population of 1897 there were 173 Jewish gentlemen and honorary citizens; 190 peasants; 1,208 merchants; 47,446 petty bourgeois estimated in Chisinau. So, all those people, as well as your relatives, obviously belonged to petty bourgeois. By the way, bookkeepers were prepared at the Jewish College of General Education opened in 1838." There had been a Jewish Library with 1,500 volumes, and in 1903, the year of the pogrom, the "Society of Art Lovers was organized and 10 Jewish artists were signed in." Olga marked this addendum with "N.B.!"

On my second visit, I slowly reimagined the city, the world inhabited by my grandparents in the years before they left for America, as a place where Jews like them lived in a style far removed from the shtetl culture they had already put behind them.

The album.

My sister does not share my fascination with the dead, but occasionally she indulges me and listens to my anecdotes about our ancestors. After my first trip to Kishinev, she mentioned that she had found an album with several photographs of our grandmother. Neither of us could remember why she instead of me had kept the album, since I had become the family archivist. It wasn't exactly a photo album, although it contained almost thirty pictures, but what else to call it? A memory book, a cross between a scrapbook and an album.

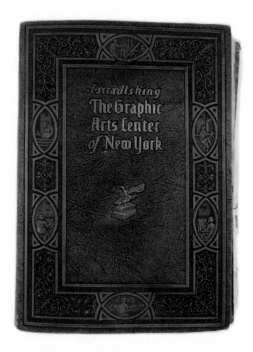

My grandmother's album was a promotional brochure, bound
in leatherette, with ten illustrated pages on expensive stock, published by the Graphic Arts Center of New York. The elaborate
self-publication announced the creation of the center in Lower Manhattan, set to open in 1927 (now an elegant twelve-story building
at 200 Varick Street). Attached to the pages with paper clips were
snapshots, as well as thick cabinet cards from Russia, Argentina,
and the Lower East Side. As we turned the heavy but now fragile
pages, I recognized my grandmother's sister from Argentina, her
husband and daughters, her sister from Canada and her nieces,
but no one else. Not one of the photographs was labeled or dated.
I slowly started to remember that I had opened this album at the
time of my father's death, but I had reluctantly closed the book
with the same sense of puzzlement that I had felt when faced with

the 1906 Kipnis family portrait. Who were these people—families, babies, groups of women, in twos and threes—important enough for my grandmother to want to remember?

Two of the studio cards from Russia were, it turned out, from my grandparents' friends in Kishinev. More at ease in the photographer's studio than my grandparents seemed to be, the elegantly turned-out friends look unafraid, prepared to enter the world on their terms. On the backs of their portraits my grandparents' friends have inscribed messages of farewell: "To my dear friend R. Kipnis and his wife, from G. and E. Frein. Remember us fondly." The Frein's one child stands between mother and father—a girl dressed in an exquisitely pleated white dress. The other signed card is by an outright dandy, whose delicately shaped mustache and fair, styled hair make him look ready for a role in an Oscar Wilde comedy: "To my friend Rafael Kipnis. Remember Y. Kaufman, January 14, 1906. P.S. My address is Kishinev, poste restante Y.K. #18." Their faces and words tell me that far from the caricatures of the dummies, the friends of Raphael and his wife belonged to a circle of people who knew there was a future beyond the pogroms. Two months later, Raphael, Sheyndel, and Shulem sail for America. Their friends would remember them. Perhaps the friends had already left.

The photographs from the dear friends, their touching gesture of farewell, confirmed to me what I had traveled to find but hadn't: something beyond the ship's manifest and beyond the family portrait that would tell me how they lived. That's why I had to return. My second trip to Kishinev was not so much to revisit the site of the pogrom, as to discover the place that my grandparents had inhabited and then left as members of that vast middle class Olga had described. The tenements of Stanton Street must have been something of a comedown for the upwardly mobile Bessarabian Kipnises, if they had resided anywhere near their friend Mr. Samuel Grigory Traub, "in his private dwelling house . . . in the upper, newly built part of the town." Or perhaps they had lived near the photography studio located, it says on the card stock, "near the water pump house."

In one of the articles published in the *New York Times* dated two months after the pogrom in June 1903, the reporter promotes the city to its readers with an intriguing headline: "Kishineff as a City: Far from a Bad Place to Live In, Except for a Jew." With the climate of Southern California, and famous for its plums, produce, tobacco, and wine, except for the pogrom, what's not to like? "The formation of the city is very striking and unusual. The old, or lower, town is on the banks of the river Byk, a tributary of the Dniester, and the new, or high town, is on high crags, rising in some places to nearly 500 feet above the level of the river."

Except for a Jew, except for a pogrom. It seems to me now that the curators at the center wanted to invoke not only the great pogrom but also the lineaments of a life, a life in a city that one might—*might*—not want to leave. And indeed my grandparents remained in Kishinev for three years after the pogrom, and after the pogroms that roiled Russia more widely in 1905. The exhibits try to manage the contradictions of what it meant to be Jewish in Kishinev at the turn of the twentieth century: the traditions of Orthodoxy—the dummy with his untrimmed beard and his black gabardine, the Sabbath candles, and the Purim puppets—but also the pleasures of music and art. Temporalities coexist, too: the Purim story, the pogrom, the Holocaust.

Still, by making a second trip I was enacting a gesture that I could not fully explain to myself—beyond the prompts of the novel and beyond the photographs with their messages of fond farewell. It's true that *The Lazarus Project*, with its vividly detailed visit to Kishinev, had challenged my memory; but my memory lapse was not a sufficient explanation. I could not shake the feeling that I was still missing something, and that I would somehow suffer from that failure, as would my book, unless I returned.

It was hard to resist the self-diagnosis that I had succumbed to the famous "repetition compulsion" that Freud describes in *Beyond the Pleasure Principle*. Freud analyzes a small child's attempts to master an early anxiety over loss through a game, a game that allows him to repeat, through a symbolic act, an apprehension—the fear of his mother's absence, of losing his mother—that threatens his sense of security. He throws out a spool and reels it back in, rehearsing on his own terms his fear that his mother has left and won't return to him—she has gone, but she will return. Repetition in this sense is a way for the child to master the terror of loss beyond all control through play. For those of us for whom the past feels burdened by loneliness, returning to the scene of where something was lost can seem comforting. For us, the child's game with the spool means fooling ourselves with time travel; if we cannot retrieve the past, we can go back to its places in the present. Playing with loss becomes a way to confront, often not fully consciously, what we are missing, to admit that we are missing something. Sometimes this is something literal: a document, the name of someone in an unidentified photograph, a scrap of paper, pieces of the past that we might have overlooked. But in the end, by returning to the place of loss, we acknowledge our true sadness, which is that we miss what's missing.

As I contemplated my return, I confronted a broader question that had been nagging at me from the start; this was an anxiety about the story that I was constructing to put in the place of my ignorance. I had experienced this uncertainty both on the site, as it were, and as I pursued my lost family at a distance, in my head and on paper, as a kind of dissatisfaction or dissonance: insufficient information, or approximate pieces of knowledge. On this second journey, I was trying to come to terms with what I still was—and would—always be missing, despite what I had found. I wanted to understand what I felt, beyond what I knew, about the effaced history of the family that I had been tracking down ever since the inheritance had entered my life. I decided to go to Israel to see the dunams my grandparents had bought, and I decided that I would return to Kishinev.

As with the first trip to meet my cousins in Memphis, I didn't have to go, but I did.

One bright summer morning on the weekend of my return visit in 2009, Natasha and I retraced our steps, by now almost familiar, on the circuit of the pogrom. Following the poem a second time, I finally began to grasp the path of the pogrom that I had missed the first time, overwhelmed by the strangeness of the topography in which I had found myself. I began to understand distances and scale, and the work of time. The River Byck, the boundary of the poorest section of the city, in 2009 was barely a rivulet. We could make out its presence only by the bridge.

We stopped to buy water at the little grocery adjacent to the famous site of House No. 13. On my previous visit I had been disappointed not to be able to enter the courtyard immortalized by Bialik, the very yard where the victims whose testimony to intimate violence Bialik and Korolenko had made known to the world. On our return to the house, staring again at the locked door, I came to realize, reluctantly, that I would have to accept the approximate evidence of the many neighboring courtyards I had already seen: close would have to be enough.

As my quest drew to a close, I wanted to name the persistent sense of a gap between my desire and the things I was desperate to discover that had characterized the journey all along. The properties of the spline had helped me map the open spaces of my beginnings; I turned now to another mathematical object in order to describe this feeling of frustration. Asymptotic: not meeting, not falling together. As plotted on a graph, an asymptote is a line that a curve forever approaches. The curve and the line look as though they will ultimately meet, but in the end, they never touch. Nicely for me, the word "symptom" shares the root of this term, which makes a kind of circular logic. My symptom was my frustration at what would not fall together.

Giving up on finding any further evidence for my grandparents' sojourn in Kishinev was harder than relinquishing the goal of seeing a space and an event made indelible by words—Bialik's poem. But recognizing that I was never going to repair that missed encounter, however belatedly, I embraced the pleasures of the proximate, in the present. On that last day in the city, Natasha,

Olga, and I instead set out to follow the clues to the addresses on the back of the photograph of my grandparents' friends. We walked past the street where one of the city's two water pumps was located, where the water pump was no more and where the friends, who were already missing my grandparents, even before their departure from Kishinev, had lived. The treasure hunt without the treasure.

At a farewell visit to the Patisserie Française, a two-story, glass-fronted café that felt almost Parisian, Natasha introduced me to Genia Brick, an expert on the history of the country starting from the medieval period, Jews in Moldova, the city of Kishinev, the pogrom, the politics of Bialik's poem. His knowledge of Jewish life was encyclopedic, and I took copious notes, but could he help me resolve my personal question of origins?

As I told my story, I drew a map on a paper napkin that sketched the journey that I concluded my grandparents must have made, arriving at Kishinev from Bratslav. I asked the historian hesitantly if he thought it was legitimate to conclude from the archival evidence about my great-grandfather's cousins that my grandparents, too, had indeed lived in Kishinev, if only for a few years, and that therefore in some way our family came from there, from here. Did that make sense? "Of course," came the reply, unhesitatingly and in English. Families were close; they chose to live near each other when they could. How close was close enough?

That persistent feeling of almost but not quite—back to back, side by side, the almost there of the asymptote—was what had disappointed me initially, on the first trip, when the archivist showed me records from my great-grandfather's cousins. I had wanted archival details for Rafael and Sheyndel; instead I had to make do with their second cousins. Now seen sideways, like the lateral roots of the banyan tree, the in-laws, the second cousins, once removed, were bringing me home. I didn't have to go that far back to understand the importance of second cousins, of distant relations: hadn't Brownie brought me closer to cracking the codes of the Kipnis enigma than I had ever been?

At the moment, I couldn't explain to myself why the historian's comment about Jewish family migration patterns—his "of course"—felt so piercingly true. After all, it was a generalization that told me nothing specific about my family tree. And yet it did. And why should this have been so surprising? All along I had been able to piece together the Kipnis puzzle through the bonds that tied them to others of their generation and their emigration. That's what the museum exhibits were designed to show—an average Jewish home at the time of the pogrom. But my grandparents were also different—the average Jewish home represented by the dummies was not theirs either. That was the bind.

No matter what I found, no matter how much history I grasped, I was still going to have to acknowledge how much had been permanently lost in transmission. I was still lacking a way to reclaim a passage back to what their years in Kishinev—the years of the photographs—had meant to them, could have meant to my father, and could, filtered through the years of their American experience, finally mean to me.

Sholem Aleichem's "Two Anti-Semites" recounts the train journey of Max Berlliant, a traveling salesman, whose work takes him all over Russia. According to the narrator, who apologizes for the phrase, Max "looks so Jewish." Poor Max, his eyes are "dark and shining, his hair the same. It's real Semitic hair. He speaks Russian like a cripple, and," Aleichem writes, "God help us, with a Yiddish singsong. And on top of everything, he's got a nose! A nose to end all noses." Max has given up all pretense of maintaining Kosher laws and other religious dictates (he eats lobster, while on the road). At the same time, the narrator explains, no matter how hard Max tries to pass (even buying the infamous newspaper *The Bessarabian*, published by the evil Krushevan and responsible for stirring up anti-Semitic feelings in the city), his performance is a failure. "You can pick him out like a counterfeit coin in a handful of change."

Unfortunately for Max, one day his job forces him to travel to Bessarabia, the region in which Kishinev was located. He has already heard about the pogroms, "a thousand horror stories about Kishinev in his home town . . . atrocities such as never had been known or heard before." The closer the train draws to Kishinev, the more his heart contracted with fear and anguish: "Max knew he was bound to meet people in these parts eager to talk about the pogroms." He doesn't want to hear the "wails and groans of those who had lost their near and dear" or the "righteous exhortations and malicious remarks of the Gentiles." He longs to escape this confrontation, and he cannot. Even in his dreams, he hears "cries and echoes of '*Ki-shi-nev*' sounded from afar." In this rare case Aleichem insists on geographical and historical accuracy. The city is locatable in the atlas, not the folkloric landscape of the storyteller, and pogroms are not given over to irony. Whatever Max's dogged efforts to pass in anti-Semitic Russia, the Kishinev pogroms defeat him. He is forced to identify with the victims: "Max was as ashamed of what had happened in Kishinev as if he was personally responsible for it, almost as if Kishinev was part of himself."

The tale takes an odd twist when a second traveler boards the train—this one a great storyteller, "a Jew like other Jews" and who "loves Jews" and jokes—and enters Max's compartment while Max is asleep. He decides to trick Max into revealing his Jewishness (deduced by evidence of Max's substantial nose) by whistling the tune of a well-known Yiddish folk song. Max spontaneously picks up the tune and sings along with his new travel companion.

Despite the fanciful invention of the doubling, the story has nothing of the comic world of Sholem Aleichem characters, of their cows, goats, and daughters to marry. This surprisingly dark tale, written in 1905, offers a way to understand that before the Holocaust came to shatter the world, Kishinev stood as the real and symbolic event of what it meant to be a Jew in Europe.

By the second time I toured the library with Olga, I had started to wonder whether there wasn't an unconscious association between Purim and pogrom in Kishinev. Purim is the story, you might say, of a thwarted pogrom. The good outcome of Purim, in which the Jews outwit their persecutors, is what should have, or could have, happened during the pogrom of 1903. There's even a visual connection between the villain Haman and evil-doer Krushevan, whose newspaper regularly published damaging reports against the Jews of Kishinev, and who is described in Hemon's novel as "the rabid anti-Semite, with his pointy beard and curled mustache and the calm, confident demeanor of someone wielding the power of life and death." In fact, that portrait fits the classic version of Haman to a tee.

A childhood melody floated back to me, irresistibly: "Oh once there was a wicked, wicked man, and Haman was his name, sir. He would have murdered all the Jews, but they were not to blame sir. Oh today, we'll merry merry be, oh today . . ." I remember that song—I could sing it now, though only this first verse, which ends with "and nosh some Hamantashan"—just as I can see my pale-eyed, dark-haired sister bedecked as Queen Esther.

She remembers her dress, "a beautiful light blue dress with gold trim." Some "filmy, Middle Eastern material," she adds. And she remembers one of the boys playing Haman, with "a big black phony mustache." And Hamantashan, those Purim cookies in the form of Haman's three-cornered hat, with teeth-blackening poppy-seed filling in the center. Is it an accident that the most delicious thing I ate in Moldova was cheesecake with a poppy-seed center at the Patisserie Française, a very un-French combination, but so very familiar? More and more, I've come to think that the Purim puppets were meant to invoke the fantasy of rescue, especially since most of those who remained did not escape their fate, Queen Esther notwithstanding.

Maybe I've been seduced into analogy by my grandfather's Purimspiel, his fantasia of liberation.

Olga left the room we had been standing in, a small performance space for the children's theatrical productions, saying she would be back, saying something, I thought, about "doors." She smiled mischievously; I waited. She returned carrying three colorfully painted dolls the size of small children (what I would have called puppets). The dolls were none other than Hemon's dummies, the Orthodox Jewish couple and an additional one, their daughter. Arranging the dolls on chairs around a small table covered with a festive cloth, and set with candlesticks, and a ceremonial kiddush cup, Olga quickly reconfigured the scene that had been the centerpiece of the exhibit I had missed, against the backdrop of a painting representing a Kishinev streetscape from the era of the pogrom.

I cannot know what I would have made of this scene had I encountered it, as Hemon had, in the center on my first visit. But as Olga, a Jewish mother of grown children, waltzed with Ora, the Jewish daughter doll, I felt pierced by the poignant effort, palpable throughout the spaces of the library, to keep the past alive. For the time of the dance, the distance between past and present collapsed, and along with it my anxiety, like the balloons wilting on the stage behind the dolls. I had been working too hard at all of this, my compulsion to document, to find the exact spot, to keep returning until I got it right. Maybe as a good daughter of Freud, my anxiety subsided because the dolls brought me back to something familiar, memories of a Jewish childhood. Maybe what I've been trying to accomplish all this time is a way to recapture the feeling of the history that only now I can acknowledge has shaped me all along.

I've inherited Purim and pogroms, but also emigration and, like Max Berlliant, the wounds to the heart as well as the real Semitic hair.

Will this have been my last pilgrimage? As I headed for the airport at Chisinau, I felt that something had settled in me, the compulsion had loosened its hold. I knew so much more than when I had begun, and yet there was so much I would never know. Having made the second trip, however, I can, for the first time, begin to admit what I was really missing, and how far I have come to knowing that.

In the final pages of his memoir *The Lost*, Daniel Mendelsohn stands in the place he had been looking for, tracking down, hoping, often hopelessly, to find: the place in a tiny village, Bolechow, where, during the Holocaust, his two relatives, Shmiel and Frydka, lost to him, had been killed. And standing there, next to the tree in the garden where they had been shot, Mendelsohn tries to say what exactly he felt at the end of his long journey. "There is so much that will always be *impossible to know*," he writes, "but we do know that they were, once, themselves, *specific*, the subjects of their own lives and deaths." But in almost the same breath, he recognizes that having found Shmiel and Frydka, or rather the closure of their stories, he would have to "give them up again, let them be themselves, whatever that had been."

I've had to settle in my own journey for representations of past lives at several removes from such concrete identification—the exact spot. Yet I've come to accept, even enjoy, my mediated knowledge: a photograph of my grandparents taken in a photography studio that no longer exists, and a home address, not theirs but that of their friends, friends whose relationship was established in a handwritten farewell inscribed on the back of yet another photograph taken at another photography studio that has also disappeared.

What I had hoped to find on this return continued to elude me. But if Kishinev beyond the poem and beyond the pogroms lacked the story I was seeking, it had become the origin of the story I would write.

17. The Order Book

*For even things lost in a house abide, like forgotten sorrows and incipient
dreams, and many household things are of purely sentimental value, like
the dim coil of thick hair, saved from my grandmother's girlhood, which
was kept in a hatbox on top of the wardrobe, along with my mother's
gray purse. In the equal light of disinterested scrutiny such things are
not themselves. They are transformed into pure object, and are horrible,
and must be burned.*

For we had to leave. | Marilynne Robinson, *Housekeeping*

What can I do about my attachment to the things that, over so many
years, have accumulated in the drawer? I'm going to have to get rid
of them eventually, but I resist the violence their disposal would
entail. As the narrator of Marilynne Robinson's novel observes,
when you start seeing the things that once had sentimental value
as "pure object" you must burn them—leave the precious objects
behind so that you can move on. Household things have a way of
hanging on, keeping you back, cathected as they are to their past
owners. We are always somehow the second savers, the keepers
of the memories of others. And yet, in the real world, it's not
feasible to burn the family house down in order to make a run
for your life, leaving the ghosts of the past behind.

Some objects are harder to dispose of than others. Soon after my father's death, as I inspected the various drawers of the family apartment, I came upon a royal-blue velvet bag embroidered with Hebrew letters, containing tefillin and tallis, in a small mahogany desk in the living room. To whom did this all belong, these traces of religious observance? My father might have received a tallis bag at the time of his bar mitzvah. I remembered somewhere a tiny snapshot of him, with another boy, wearing a tallis and a fedora at about the right age. But while the smooth fabric of the bag looked to be of more recent vintage, I could conjure no memory of seeing my father take the bag out of the drawer, wear the tallis it contained, or carry the bag with him, even on the high holidays when he and my mother went to temple. Certainly I never saw him "lay" tefillin, as the canonical expression goes. I moved back a generation: my unmet grandfather's? Although the tefillin's leather was stiff and dry to the touch, the bag's surface did not look worn. Perhaps it had spent most of its life in the drawer.

Because the paraphernalia of prayer belongs to men, I could not see the point in saving this legacy, but something about putting the velvet bag in the trash along with the household garbage made me uneasy—would I be throwing away an entire tradition? Part of me said, yes, and why not? As a woman, I had no use for any of it. But because I also knew something about the meaning of tefillin (to simplify, a symbolic reminder of what binds Jews to God), I balked, superstitiously, I admit, at just unloading the whole leather contraption, straps and all. Instead, I arrived at a compromise with myself. I opened the outside container, thus satisfying my curiosity about what was inside, and preserved the two small boxes hidden within.

Divested of the straps and the external container, as objects the little, embossed, brown-leather cubes (one and a half inches in height, depth, and width), tiny boxes lined with velvet and stamped with Hebrew letters in green, have a certain wistful, antique charm. I would save them, I decided, as a souvenir of my father's abandoned religious past, along with two objects I knew he valued: his Phi Beta Kappa key, which had dangled from the gold chain attached to his pocket watch, and the watch itself, which rested on a little bronze stand. The cubes, minus the prayers inscribed on paper they originally contained, would remain on my desk as a stand-in for the mysteries I would never solve but to which I was distantly connected. The empty leather boxes join a selection of framed family photographs and other sentimental objects that now sit on my desk in a kind of private museum: the photograph of my grandparents and uncle in Kishinev, the portrait of my great-aunt Zirl, the postcard of my uncle Sam in his World War I uniform, a handmade ceramic mezuzah decorated by the children at the JCC in Kishinev, and my grandfather's silver cigarette case.

The quest for knowledge feeds on itself, creates cravings for more. For instance, when I found the origin of the many snapshots of my father's athletic and military exertions, which turned out to have been the visual record of a summer spent at a Citizens Training Camp in 1927, I did not know what my father had done in the years between graduation from De Witt Clinton High School and entering Brooklyn Law School. It bothered me not to know, but I set the question aside, as I had set aside many such ancillary matters, as a problem I could not resolve, or didn't need to solve, or didn't think was essential to solve, or else I pretended I didn't care. What difference did it make, really? Considering the many holes in my story, the huge gaps in chronology, the lost archives, this little missing piece was, or should have been, a minor irritation. Wasn't it just a sidebar?

But one day, as I was nearing the end of what I had come to acknowledge was the story as far as I would ever know it, a nagging impulse made me think that if only I obtained my father's transcript from City College (I knew that he had ultimately graduated from there in 1947), I might be able to fill in that blank in his narrative. Although there are legal obstacles to acquiring someone else's transcript, even if the other person is your father, thanks to the intervention of a colleague who worked his insider magic at his home institution, within a day of inquiring I received by e-mail both the transcript and a note from the registrar. I stared in wonder at this public document, with all the information filled in by hand.

The registrar explained what at first glance looked confusing. "He actually took more than four years to complete," she wrote, describing my father's history as a student. "He started in the spring semester of 1925 and with continuous attendance through spring of 1927. . . . He took three courses at Brooklyn Law School; he then returned in Spring of 1942 . . . with continuous attendance through fall of 1946. . . . He completed 132.5 credits and graduated at the end of fall 1946 with degree date of Feb. 1, 1947." My father graduated cum laude, after four years in night school, the two segments separated by more than two decades.

The transcript revealed something very important about my father's path to education, but it also brought an unexpected return to a childhood memory of being alone with my father, a memory I had never been able to date. It was the spring semester of 1946, in a course in geology. My father would have been thirty-nine, and I would have been five, in kindergarten. I feel as if I have always remembered this experience for it has the quality of a dream, which is the only way I can retell it. The trip must have been to the Palisades, and the students told that they could bring their kids. I remember looking for mica, easy to spot as it glinted on granite cliffs (that might be another memory from playing in Central Park, but I did know what mica was, I think), near a place where there was water, maybe the Hudson River, if it was the Palisades, or a nearby lake. We had not brought a bathing suit for the excursion, and so my father let me wade into the water in my underpants. That was fun, but then I had wet underpants for the return home (I must have been wearing a skirt or a dress). What to do? Stretching the two sides of my undershirt down as far as they could go, my father attached them together with a large safety pin, which meant that the safety pin was lodged between my legs. I remember coming home happy after my great adventure with my father (Junior Miss Oedipus) and hearing my mother berate him mercilessly upon discovering his "solution" to my wet underpants. All the terrible things that could have befallen me had the safety pin opened. What could he have been thinking?

The memory of that scene flooded back to me intact the moment I ran my eye over the transcript entries. Geology 1, 3 credits, B. That girl, her father, her mother, me.

So in the end—after all my questing, hunting, searching, researching in Ukraine and Moldova, looking for what had come down to me from my father, I retrieve instead one of my oldest childhood memories, an intensely private moment weirdly tethered to a public document.

The transcript also revealed the material evidence of something more intimate than this memory or the love letters between my parents, something I had suspected but never understood during my childhood: the class difference between my parents, or rather between their families of origin. The transcript sends back to me the reflection of not the father I knew, not even the father of my childhood, the father who might once have draped a tallis over his shoulders, but rather the earlier incarnation of my father as an immigrant, which he almost was, the accidental American, the father somehow hidden from view by the acquired manners of assimilation.

The transcript moves me back in time from his graduation from City College in 1947, to his first courses in 1925, and then finally to an undated photograph, a snapshot of my infant father fashioned, by its cardboard frame, to look like a studio portrait, my father, the prominent Kipnis ears already on display, swaddled in his metal carriage, posed in a street, next to a subway grate. The trace of a woman standing against the brick wall, his mother perhaps, prevents us from thinking he's just been abandoned there, but he looks as lost as his brother does in the Kishinev portrait; both boys' eyebrows frown upward, forming a kind of question mark of confusion. Seen together, the brothers are joined in an anxiety about their existence in the world. Matting the snapshot meant that the photograph could have a semi-public existence, propped on a mantelpiece, for instance. Maybe the parents were proud of their American-born son.

Scanned, the photo reveals a bluish tint, which suggests that it's a gelatin silver print, typical of the period. This one, the earliest photograph of my father, is one of very few (one posed studio photograph holding a faux violin when he was about two)—not even a handful before he reached adolescence. My father never composed an album for himself. He doesn't appear in his mother's improvised album of her side of the family. But I have collected the elements of an album or a scrapbook; I'm left now hoping that I've created one for him.

If my father was the first American in his family, my mother was the last child of four, three American siblings preceded her entrance into the world. My grandfather Miller made enough

money in his tailoring shop to provide for his children's college
and professional educations, music lessons, vacations, and ambitions. They lived on the Upper West Side, not the Lower East Side.
The Kipnis grandparents, by comparison, were poorer relations.

The transcript made visible the portrait of my father through
the eyes of a public official, who had seen many others. My father
had obtained a college education like a person from a working-
class family, or like an immigrant: at night, and while he worked.
My mother had sailed through Hunter College, attending classes
during the day, graduating early, with time to play the violin in
the school orchestra, pictured in her album, even if, as she had
told us many times, she and her sister had had to work at various
part-time jobs (the famous envelope-addressing) to contribute to
the fancier education of their oldest brother. And then, after the
war, despite the demands of a law career and family responsibilities, my father decided to return to finish his college degree. He
didn't need the degree for any material reason that I can fathom,
but he must have been motivated by a symbolic one. When I think
back to the early letters between my mother and father, and my
father's allusions to Descartes, it strikes me that his assertion of
superiority (which of them had the better translation? He did,
of course, even if she was the French major) masked an insecu-
rity about my mother's precocity, skipping grades, graduating at
nineteen. The last grade entered on the City College transcript
was an A in philosophy.

Growing up, I failed to register this sliver of social difference
between the sides as such, in part because the Kipnises were almost
entirely absent, in part because the Millers' numbers and noise
pushed my father's family history even further into obscurity.
And then my father's role as a lawyer, a member of a professional,
educated class, mooted that original distinction. What made my

parents seem different from each other was above all, as it played out in scenes of family life, one of temperament. But as a couple in the 1950s, seen from our eyes as children and adolescents, my parents together radiated well-being and prosperity, even though they never were, my mother thought, well-off enough.

It's perhaps their hard-won middle classness that explains my father's perplexity, as we sat drinking vodka in the kitchen, when I told him I was leaving my job teaching at Barnard College—where I had also gone to school—to become part of the faculty at the City University. If I had gone forward, beyond my parents, as they had moved past theirs, by degrees—getting a PhD at Columbia—wasn't linking my fate to the system that had given both my mother and him their credentials (his cherished Phi Beta Kappa key) a dangerous step downward on the ladder of upward mobility?

The family novel from which we each descend continues to haunt us into late life, embarrassing us with its revelations and disappointments, as well as with its intractable plots (intractable because they are behind us, already played out). It strikes me, for instance, having completed the voyage of the names that I've been tracking from the objects that they are attached to, that if I am at the end of the paternal line, I'm equally situated in last place at the end of the maternal line. Both sides end with me. That recognition makes me want to bring the two strands together in some final gesture of reconciliation, since I belong to both. But when I look for Miller objects to collect on the desk of my museum, I'm surprised to notice that despite the overwhelming role of the Miller grandparents in my life when they were alive, I have almost no objects with which to install their presence now, nothing but my grandmother's bronze Sabbath candlesticks that a Miller cousin gave me a decade ago when her mother—my mother's sister—died. I've had bad luck with the only two other Miller family objects once in my possession: a small diamond belonging to my mother's mother that I gave to my stepson's fiancée, who subsequently vanished into China, her country of origin, minus the husband but keeping the ring; and a delicate eighteen-carat gold watch set with tiny rubies that I gave to the lovely young woman with a slender wrist who married a Miller cousin's son—another marriage headed for dissolution.

It is time to learn something from my bad luck with heirlooms. What anyway am I trying to pass on, pass down? I may hope that in the absence of children of my own, these physical, material mementos will somehow keep me alive in the memory of future generations after my death—but they are only so tenuously me, mine, that I should probably not be counting on them to carry that burden. The pair of candlesticks, for instance, the one Miller household thing still mine. I had no idea, until they were handed over to me after the unveiling of my aunt's headstone, that they existed in my cousin's possession, just waiting to be transmitted to someone else in the family, in this case, me. I've promised them to another cousin's son. I can't say that I see in memory my maternal grandmother—his great-grandmother—lighting Sabbath candles. If I'm being truthful, I'm compelled to admit that it's an effort on my part to endow the candlesticks with meaning after the fact, although I'm quite happy to have them as reminders of what I do not remember.

Like the empty tefillin boxes, the candlesticks once embodied a living tradition, but unlike the boxes, with which I do not pray, I occasionally feel moved to light the candles on a Friday night as a gesture of connection. Perhaps like the Kipnis silverware, the candlesticks, too, traveled from Russia, and they tie me by a symbolic thread to that inherited past of untold stories. Still, given my place at the end of the line, there is no next generation who will inherit from me; I end up an heiress minus heirs, no next generation except if I move sideways on the tree—a lesson about new object relations that I have trouble retaining. But if I'm stuck with my objects unless they become recognizable paper shapes—Jewish origami?—I've at least made that move outward to the readers who share the dilemma of uncertain origins and unrootedness, and wasn't that the point of the journey?

Toward the end of *A Woman's Story*, a family memoir composed after her mother's death, Annie Ernaux describes an unexpected conversation with an aunt who reveals an intimate detail about her parents' love life, from the time of their courtship. "Now that my mother is dead," Ernaux writes, "I wouldn't want to learn anything about her that I hadn't known when she was alive." When I read the memoir several years ago, I was struck by the remark: why would you not want to continue discovering things about the past, reinterpreting earlier visions? Now, as I come close to finishing my own book, I find myself drawn to her resistance. Soon, I am not going to want to know more—about my parents, about my grandparents, about any of them: the ancestors. Every new piece of information keeps me on the road to the ever-expanding possibility of the quest, a quest that in the end will still yield only partial knowledge—and will never give me, return to me, those past lives. That seems obvious, and didn't I know that from the start? That they would never return to me? Yes, but the lure of the puzzle, the enigma of lineage—who *were* these people—is not so easily resisted. Only weeks ago, Alla, my genealogist in Kishinev, sent me new entries for Kipnis names, promising still more from Odessa. So, soon, I'll stop, but not yet. The sirens of genealogy have a song all their own, backed up by the ceaseless music of the Internet.

I was about to end there, on a note of journey's end, an accounting of loss, somewhat melancholic, but also an inventory, rather more sanguine, of all that has been found. I was searching for a metaphor of closure that would balance out the lost and the found. But as I prepared to close the book on the family quest, the door to the past reopened—so conveniently that it borders on fiction. Almost exactly one year after my trip to Tucson, the scrapbook that my uncle deposited in the library at the University of Arizona suddenly materialized. The head of Special Collections had been working in the backlog of unprocessed materials and came upon the Kipnis donation. Out of the blue, an envelope with copies of most of the scrapbook's contents arrived on my doorstep, as if by magic. I remembered looking back longingly at the huge filing cabinet labeled "unprocessed" as we left the library empty-handed and disappointed, wondering whether my uncle's scrapbook could possibly be there and wishing we could rummage through the files still in limbo. But my uncle's materials had been placed in a folder and the folder in an envelope; even if we had been allowed to search we might have missed our chance to triumph, since stored in that fashion the scrapbook in no way resembled the object we had visualized.

The scrapbook was in fact an ordinary business item, seven inches wide by eleven inches long, with ruled lines and columns for calculating figures—an order book, very much like the ledger that my grandfather had used to sketch out the family tree. Just as my grandmother had converted the pages of a publicity brochure into a photograph album, my uncle had repurposed the ledger as a scrapbook, a holder of memorabilia.

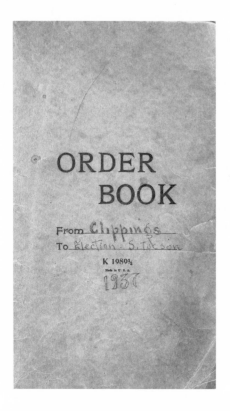

A ledger invites accountability. Looking at the scanned image of my uncle's scrapbook pinned to the bulletin board above my desk, I remembered the ledger I bought when I started taking notes for my dissertation. I wanted something different from my graduate-student notebooks for this new departure. The narrower boundaries of the pages and their columns helped me organize my inchoate beginnings. My boyfriend at the time, an illustrator, marked the occasion by drawing on the blank front page of the ledger a picture of me sitting at my desk with my hair in a huge Afro (it was the seventies, after all), hands thrown up with amazement as my cat madly types the pages that come flying out of my typewriter. Long after we split up, I had the drawing framed; I show it to my students when they worry whether their pages will add up to a dissertation.

With my uncle's order book, I closed a circle in memory that reconnected me to a family practice, and to a family of keepers.

There were few biographical surprises, since the donation receipt had enumerated most of the archive's contents. But the details were acutely rewarding—illuminating my uncle's World War I service (he hadn't lied, as I had feared, in his newspaper interview about learning to fly in the Army Air Corps), and revealing his local political ambitions before the mayoral adventure (a letter in reply from the Democratic National Committee about "The Sahuaro Club" Sam seemed to have created). Beyond the specifics of the documentation—the letters, the clippings about his career in South Tucson, the snapshots from Call Field, the base in Texas he had helped build in 1917—was the bittersweet taste of the finding itself, which in so many ways embodied the turns of the quest over the years. There was the sought-after object—but still requiring a return journey.

I could not quite coincide with the thing itself—and, moreover, the thing itself was not the thing itself. At the same time, something of all that had been lost had been found, and I consoled myself with the thought that sometime in the near future I would return to Tucson, descend into the domain of Special Collections, and take the scrapbook in my hand. I've studied copies of the clippings and photographs once glued to its pages, so I'm forewarned that I won't find there the explanation for what happened between the brothers.

I still long to know what I'm missing.

The order book was a reminder, if I needed one, that the past continues to reshape our ideas of who we are in the present. That's also why we find it so difficult to stop our excavations: the archeology of ancestry reveals as much about us as it does about the beings lost to us in time.

Would I remain, then, forever suspended between lost and found? Was that the final lesson of the scrapbook's belated reappearance, turning up just when I was sure that no further discoveries could affect the dénouement of my quest? For now I would remain, it seemed, where I had already arrived, but as we know, a story about finding always returns to the places where the story got lost. It's also a chance to begin again.

Acknowledgments

Every book is a collaboration, but some more than others. I am grateful to the many readers who have been part of this project: Natasha Alhazov, Marta Bladek, Mikhal Dekel, Marianne DeKoven, Sarah Frieden, Sarah Glazer, Susan Gubar, Annabel Herzog, Tamar Hess, Marianne Hirsch, Gloria Jacobs, Irene Kacandes, Wayne Koestenbaum, David Lazar, Jennifer Lemberg, Lorie Novak, Donald Petrey, Sandy Petrey, Jay Prosser, Victoria Rosner, Mathilde Roussel-Giraudy, Alix Kates Shulman, Olga Sivac, Leo Spitzer, Sara Jane Stoner, Ronna Texidor, and Kamy Wicoff.

I owe a special debt to Cecelia Cancellaro, my agent and senior development editor, who saw the book through with grace and finesse.

I thank Frances Bailey, amateur genealogist of the Kipnis name, for her years of knowledgeable research advice as I traced my missing family members. I thank Mathilde Roussel-Giraudy for her photo editing, for her expertise in all things visual, and not least for designing my classy family tree. Natasha Alhazov guided me through Moldova and Ukraine with ingenuity and patience. Olga Sivac taught me what it might have meant to live in Kishinev at the turn of the twentieth century. Alla Chastina traced my ancestors in that city's archive.

Still other debts impossible to repay.

Sarah Castleberry's stories about the family I had found in the drawer brought the past alive and also enlivened the present. Warren Platt, the expert genealogist at the New York Public Library, neatly solved many of what appeared to be our intractable Kipnis mysteries. Tamar Hess brought me precious access to my grandmother's property in Israel and its backstory; Ruth Kark's scholarship illuminated the local geography of my legacy. Alan Miller graciously oversaw the contractual arrangements of the inheritance at the heart of this story.

I am grateful to Lynne Collins, whose savvy research uncovered, among other family things, my uncle's story in the Southwest.

Chana Pollack and Myra Mniewski translated the Talmud Torah letters and the snapshot messages, and Miriam Hoffman translated the letter from Argentina.

Since the journey of this book began with objects found in a drawer, I am happily indebted to the artists and photographers who created their elegant appearance in these pages: Spencer Jones (the cigarette case, the silverware) and, above all, Lorie Novak (the property map, the box of curls, my grandmother's album). The image of the order book appears with the permission of the Kipnis Collection, University of Arizona Library, Special Collections. I am grateful to Roger Myers and Chrystal Carpenter of Special Collections for their assistance.

For editorial assistance during manuscript preparation I thank Marta Bladek, Sara Jane Stoner, and Vina Tran.

I want to thank The Memorial Foundation for Jewish Culture for generously supporting the project of this book. I would also like to express my appreciation to the Warner Fund at the University Seminars at Columbia University for their help in publication. Material in this work was presented to the University Seminar: Cultural Memory. A psc-cuny research grant facilitated my travel to Eastern Europe and Israel.

Not least, I wish to thank Kristen Elias Rowley, my editor at University of Nebraska Press, for her critical tact throughout the process, her assistant Courtney Ochsner for help in bringing the manuscript to book form, and Sara Springsteen for her thoughtful finishing touches.

Earlier versions of chapters 4, 7, 15, and 16 appeared in the following publications and are used with permission: "I Killed My Grandmother: Mary Antin, Amos Oz, and the Autobiography of a Name," *Biography: An Interdisciplinary Quarterly* 30, no. 3 (Spring 2007): 319–41. © Biographical Research Center; "Beguiled by Loss," in *Exposed Memory: Family Pictures in Private and Collective Memory*, ed. Zsófia Bán and Hedvig Turai (Budapest: AICA, Hungarian Section, 2010); "Letter from Argentina," *Hotel Amerika* 7, no. 2 (Spring 2009): 146–51; "Family Hair Looms," *WSQ* 36, nos. 1 and 2 (Spring/Summer 2008): 162–68, published by The Feminist Press at the City University of New York; "Kishinev Redux: Pogrom, Purim, Patrimony," in *Rites of Return*, ed. Marianne Hirsch and Nancy K. Miller. © 2011 Columbia University Press. Reprinted with permission of the publisher.

Sources

1. The Heiress

7 **My grandfather Willie:** Grace Paley, "The Immigrant Story," in *The Collected Stories* (New York: Farrar, Straus and Giroux, 1999), 238.

3. The Report Card

31 **A scholarly article:** Philip J. Pauley, "The Development of High School Biology, New York City, 1900–1925," *Isis* 82, no. 4 (December 1991): 668.

4. The Photograph from Kishinev

36 **Epigraph:** Hayim Nahman Bialik, "City of the Killings," in *Songs from Bialik: Selected Poems of Hayim Nahman Bialik*, trans. Atar Hadari (Syracuse: Syracuse University Press, 2000), 1.

37 **Kopl says to me, "You don't know what a pogrom is?":** Sholem Aleichem, "Among the Emigrants," in *The Adventures of Motl the Cantor's Son*, trans. Aliza Shevrin (New York: Penguin, 2009), 242.

38 **Internationally reported:** Bialik, "City of the Killings," 1–9.

38 **Once I made the Bialik connection:** Marcel Proust, *Remembrance of Things Past*, vol. 2, trans. Scott Montcrieff and Terence Kilmartin (New York: Vintage, 1982), 108; Vladimir Nabokov, *Speak, Memory: An Autobiography Revisited* (New York: Vintage, 1989), 174.

42 **Not all the Motl stories treat the passage:** Sholem Aleichem, "Mazel Tov, We're in America," in *The Adventures of Motl the Cantor's Son*, trans. Aliza Shevrin (New York: Penguin, 2009), 288.

5. The *Nudnik* and the Boss
57 "A *nudnik*," explains Leo Rosten: Leo Rosten, *The Joys of Yiddish* (New York: McGraw-Hill, 1968), 270.

8. Wolf and Virgin
87 Reading the letters, I want to shout at them: Delmore Schwartz, "In Dreams Begin Responsibilities," in *In Dreams Begin Responsibilities and Other Stories* (New York: New Directions, 1978), 6.

9. The Mayor of South Tucson
99 In the *Smoke Signal*, another local publication: David Devine, "Struggle for Survival: The South Tucson Story, Tucson Area Incorporations, 1933–1997," *Smoke Signal*, no. 71 (Summer 2000): 4.

100 In one of his stories: Sholem Aleichem, "Tevye Blows a Small Fortune," in *Tevye the Dairyman and the Railroad Stories*, trans. Hillel Halkin (New York: Schocken Books, 1987), 21.

101 For more details, I flesh out Sarah's picture: E. L. Doctorow, *Billy Bathgate* (New York: Harper, 1990).

10. The Lost Scrapbook
122 "The shrewd-faced boy with the melancholy eyes": Hutchins Hapgood, *The Spirit of the Ghetto* (Cambridge: Belknap Press, 1967), 18.

11. Distant Cousins
149 In *The Last Gift of Time*: Carolyn Heilbrun, *The Last Gift of Time* (New York: Dial Press, 1997), 192.

12. My Kishinev Pogrom
157 Epigraph: Amy Bloom, *Away* (New York: Random House, 2007), 58.

162 We stop in front of a one-story building: V. G. Korolenko, "House No. 13: An Episode in the Massacre of Kishinieff," *The Contemporary Review* 85 (February 1904): 279.

163 "And to the attics of the roofs you'll climb": Bialik, "City of the Killings," 1.

13. The Silverware from Russia

177 **Epigraph:** Rebecca Solnit, *A Field Guide to Getting Lost* (New York: Penguin, 2005), 59.

14. My Grandmother's Dunams

183 **Epigraph:** James Joyce, *Ulysses* (New York: Vintage, 1961), 60.

184 **Feller's brochure:** Quoted in Joseph B. Glass, *From New Zion to Old Zion: American Jewish Immigration and Settlement in Palestine, 1917–1939* (Detroit: Wayne State Press, 2002), 321–22.

15. Family Hair Looms

191 **Epigraph:** Eavan Boland, *Object Lessons: The Life of the Woman and the Poet in Our Time* (New York: W. W. Norton, 1995), 32.

193 **The next morning:** JewishGen, http://www.jewishgen.org/Yizkor/chelm/che295.html.

195 **There is, for instance, a well-known Hasidic story:** Gershom Scholem, *Major Trends in Jewish Mysticism* (New York: Schocken, 1995), 349–50.

16. Return to Kishinev

198 **Epigraph:** Alice Munro, *The View from Castle Rock* (New York: Knopf, 2006), 347.

199 **"The two of us who could never have experienced":** Aleksandar Hemon, *The Lazarus Project* (New York: Riverhead Books, 2008), 229.

206 **It was hard to resist the self-diagnosis:** Sigmund Freud, *Beyond the Pleasure Principle*, trans. James Strachey (New York: W. W. Norton, 1961), 8–11.

210 **Sholem Aleichem's "Two Anti-Semites" recounts:** Sholom Aleichem, "Two Anti-Semites," trans. Miriam Waddington, in *The Best of Sholom Aleichem*, ed. Irving Howe and Ruth R. Wisse (New York: Simon and Schuster, 1979), 115.

212 **There's even a visual connection:** Hemon, *The Lazarus Project*, 230.

214 **"There is so much that will always be *impossible to know*":** Daniel Mendelsohn, *The Lost* (New York: HarperCollins, 2006), 502.

17. The Order Book

216 **Epigraph:** Marilynne Robinson, *Housekeeping* (New York: Bantam, 1982), 209.

225 **Toward the end of *A Woman's Story*:** Annie Ernaux, *A Woman's Story*, trans. Tanya Leslie (New York: Four Walls Eight Windows, 1991), 91.